C++ FOR BEGINNERS

An Introduction to C++
Programming and Object Oriented
Programming with Tutorials and
Hands-On Examples

Table of Contents

1. Introduction

C++, pronounced as C-plus-plus (abbreviated as CPP) is a general purpose programming language which supports generic, procedural and object-oriented programming (abbreviated as OOP) paradigms. Programming paradigms are used to classify programming languages based on their features. C++ is largely influenced by C programming language and can be used to write applications for desktop, embedded systems, mobile devices, web, etc. Video games can also be developed in C++. It is a mid-level language; that is, it can be used to perform low-level system operations like memory manipulations as well as high level operations object oriented programming.

Nowadays, most of the enterprise software is built with a combination of different programming languages rather than one particular language. Some of the famous software written with the help of C++ are – *Mozilla Firefox, Google Chrome (based on Chromium browser), Apache OpenOffice, MySQL Server, VLC Media Player, etc.* In fact, *Facebook, Google, PayPal and Amazon* also make use of C++ in their server-side backend.

In 1979, a Dutch computer scientist called *Bjarne Stroustrup* started developing C++ programming language as a part of his thesis which started with developing *"C with classes"*. The first commercial implementation was released in October 1985.

Over the years, there have been a lot of improvements to the initial implementation of C++. ***International Organization for Standardization (ISO)*** standardizes C++. The first standard ***ISO/IEC 14882:1998 (C++98)*** was approved in 1998. The latest standard at the time of writing this book is ***ISO/IEC 14882:2017 (C++17)*** which was approved in 2017. Each new standard offers new features and/or improvements to the previous ones. This book follows the widely used ***ISO/IEC 14882:2011 (C++11)*** standard which was approved in 2011. Unless you are a professional core C++ developer whose life revolves around developing performance critical applications in C++, you should not be worried about the ever evolving C++ standards.

With this book, you will learn the basics of C++. The concepts of procedural programming as well as object oriented programming have been covered. Having some knowledge of programming, especially knowing C programming language will help although not necessary. However, you should be comfortable with using your PC/MAC. Some experience with the usage of Terminal of Linux/MAC and Command Prompt on Windows is needed.

2. Getting Started

A PC/Laptop with Windows/Linux operating system or an Apple Macintosh is needed to be able to develop applications in C++. A C++ program can be written and saved with the help of almost any text editor; this is known as the program source or source code. C++ source files have the extensions of - .C, .cc, .cpp, .cxx, .c++, .h, .hh, .hpp, .hxx, .h++. A source file is just another text file and needs to be converted to an executable file. This job is done by a computer software called *Compiler*. A compiler is a software that translates source code into machine-level executable code. Microsoft Visual C++, GNU Compiler Collection (GCC g++) and Clang C++ are some of the most widely used C++ compilers. Microsoft Visual C++ as the name suggests works only on Microsoft Windows operating systems. Whereas GCC and Clang work on Windows, Linux and MAC.

2.1 Environment Setup

We will be using **GCC** on a Windows PC to demonstrate programming examples in this book. The same examples will work with GCC, Clang and most other compilers on Linux and MAC too.

GCC stands for *GNU Compiler Collection* and the package has different compilers for C, C++, Ada, Fortran, etc. We will only install what we need to compile C++ programs. In the GCC package, *gcc* is the command line utility used for compiling C programs and *g++* is the command line utility for compiling C++ programs.

Any text editor including Notepad can be used to write C++ programs. I recommend a text editor called ***Notepad++*** (https://notepad-plus-plus.org/).

2.1.1 GCC Installation on Windows

MinGW (http://www.mingw.org/) and ***Cygwin*** (https://sourceware.org/cygwin/) projects provide the official ports of GCC for Windows. We will be using MinGW. MinGW, a short form for "*Minimalist GNU for Windows*", is a minimalist development environment for Windows applications. To download MinGW, visit: https://sourceforge.net/projects/mingw/files/ and download the latest installation file. Once downloaded, execute the installation file. This file will install the MinGW Installation Manager Setup Tool and not MinGW directly.

The following window should be launched once the installation file is executed:

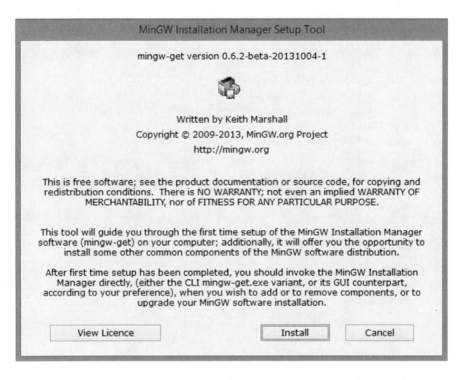

Click **Install** and you will be taken to the next window:

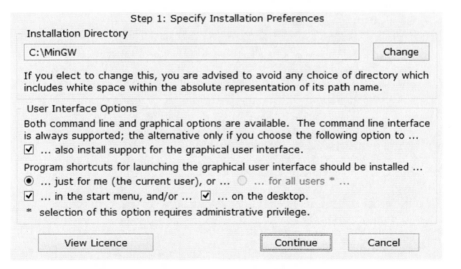

Make sure the installation directory is easily accessible, do not change any other options; click **Continue.**

The setup process will now download all the required files; this may take a few minutes. After all files are fetched, the installation window will look like this:

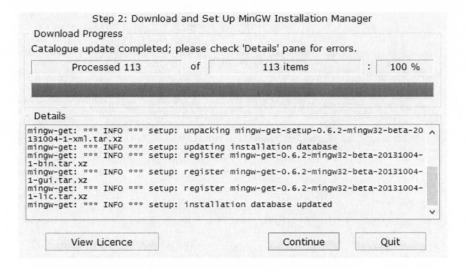

Click **Continue** and the *MinGW Installation Manager* should start. This is where you will install the **GCC** compiler.

Click the check box next to ***mingw32-gcc-g++***, click Mark for Installation. Click ***Installation -> Apply Changes*** from the menu bar. The installation process of GCC (g++) compiler will now start and may take a few minutes to finish.

Open *File Explorer* (or My Computer/This PC) and go to the *MinGW installation directory* (If you did not change any options during installation, it will be *C:\MinGW*), open *bin* folder and make sure that a file called *g++ (g++.exe)* is present; if so the installation is successful. The path to this bin folder (For Example, *C:\MinGW\bin*) needs to be added to the *Path environment variable* to make g++ globally accessible. To do so, open *System Properties* (Open Control Panel, search for *Advanced System Settings* in the search box and click *View advanced system settings*). Go to the *Advanced* Tab, *click Environment Variables*. Under *System Variables*, locate the variable *Path*, click *Edit*. The following box will pop up:

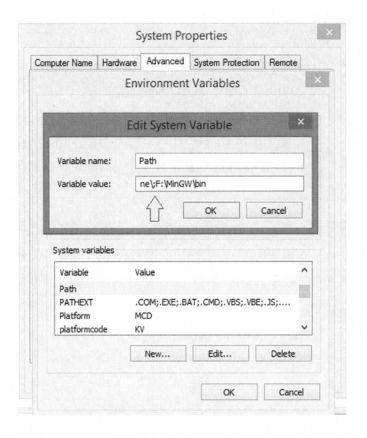

There will be some value in the **Variable value** field. Add a semi-colon (;) to the end of the text if it is not present and append the complete **MinGW\bin** path (For Example, **C:\MinGW\bin**) to it as shown in the screenshot above. Close all the boxes by clicking **OK** on by one.

Open **Command Prompt**, type **g++** and hit Enter. If you see an error like this – " **'g++' is not recognized as an internal or external command, operable program or batch file.**", there is a problem either with the installation or with the **Path** variable. In such a case follow each and every step mentioned in this section (**Section 2.1.1**) carefully. On successful installation and proper Path variable settings, the **g++** command should return the following error – "g++: fatal error: no input files compilation terminated. ".

This is what the Command Prompt will look like if the installation is successful and the Path variable has been properly set up:

2.1.2 GCC/Clang Installation on Linux

Most Linux operating systems come with GCC and/or Clang built-in. To check if your Linux OS has GCC and/or Clang, open *Terminal/Shell* and enter *g++* and *clang++* on two separate occasions.

If GCC is present, the Terminal/Shell will look like this after entering the *g++* command:

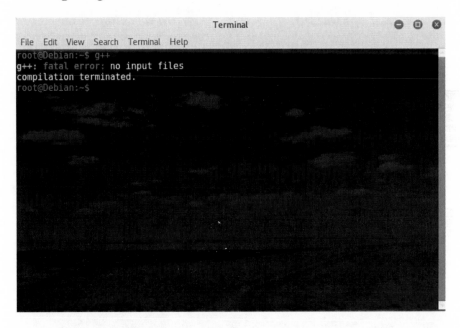

If Clang is present, the Terminal/Shell will look like this after entering the *clang++* command:

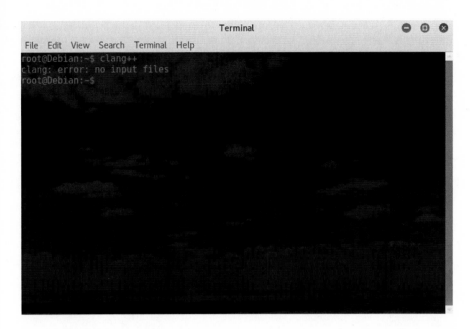

Presence of either GCC or Clang is enough to compile and execute the programs demonstrated in this book. If both compilers are absent, you will have to install either one (I recommend GCC). Installation procedure varies from OS to OS. Here are the GCC installation procedures for most common Linux Operating Systems:

For Ubuntu, Linux Mint and other Debian based systems:

Open *Terminal/Shell* and enter the following commands one by one:

```
$>sudo apt-get update
$>sudo apt-get install gcc
```

For Manjaro, Antergos and other Arch Linux based systems:

Open *Terminal/Shell* and enter the following command:

11

```
$>pacman -S gcc
```

For Fedora, CentOS and other RedHat based systems:

Open *Terminal/Shell* and enter the following command:

```
$>sudo yum install gcc-g++
```

For OpenSUSE Linux:

Open *Terminal/Shell* and enter the following command:

```
$> zypper install gcc
```

2.1.3 GCC/Clang Installation on MAC OS

The best way of installing GCC or Clang on MAC OS is to install Apple's official development suite – *Xcode*. Starting from *XCode 4.2*, the default compiler shipped with it is Clang, earlier versions will have GCC. To check whether you have GCC or Clang, open Terminal and type *g++* and *clang++* on two different occasions. The error messages shown in *Section 2.1.2* shall indicate which compiler is present. Presence of either one shall suffice.

2.2 Program Compilation and Execution

To compile a program, we must have the program source file saved with a *.cpp* extension at a convenient location. The compilation procedure remains pretty much the same for GCC and Clang across Windows, Linux and MAC.

To compile a C++ program using GCC, the following command is used:

```
g++ <source .cpp file> -o <executable output file>
eg:
g++ hello.cpp -o hello
```

To compile a C++ program using Clang, the following command is used:

```
clang++ <source .cpp file> -o <executable output file>
eg:
clang++ hello.cpp -o hello
```

If there are no errors in the source file and the compilation happens to be successful, an executable output file will be generated as specified by the **–o** option in the compile command. The executable file on Windows will automatically have the **.exe** extension. If the **–o** option is not set; i.e. no output file has been mentioned, an executable file called **a.out** will be generated on Linux/MAC and **a.exe** will be generated on Windows upon successful compilation.

In order to execute the compiled program, the following commands are used:

In Linux/MAC:

```
./<executable output file>
eg:
./hello
```

In Windows:

```
<executable output file>
eg:
hello.exe
```

Let us take an example. Open a text editor of your choice on whichever operating system, copy the following C++ code and paste it into the text editor. This code only displays *Hello World!!!* on the screen. You do not have to understand the code for now, just learn the compilation and execution procedure.

```cpp
#include <iostream>

using namespace std;

int main()
{
    cout << endl << "Hello World!!!" << endl << endl;
    return 0;

}
```

Save the file at a convenient location as *helloworld.cpp*. Open Command Prompt on Windows or Terminal on Linux/MAC. Navigate to the directory where *helloworld.cpp* has been placed using the *cd* command.

With GCC compiler on Windows, compile the code using the following command:

```
g++ helloworld.cpp -o helloworld
```

If the compilation procedure is successful, no error messages will be returned and *helloworld.exe* file will be generated:

```
┌─────────────────────────────────────────────────── CMD ─────────────── _ □ ✕ ─┐
│ F:\cpp>g++ helloworld.cpp -o helloworld                                      ^ │
│ F:\cpp>                                                                        │
│                                                                                │
│                                                                                │
│                                                                                │
│                                                                              ∨ │
└────────────────────────────────────────────────────────────────────────────────┘
```

Cross check whether *helloworld.exe* file is present using the *dir* command or by manually going to the directory using *File Explorer*. Here is the output of the *dir* command:

```
┌─────────────────────────────────────────────────── CMD ─────────────── _ □ ✕ ─┐
│ F:\cpp>g++ helloworld.cpp -o helloworld                                      ^ │
│ F:\cpp>dir                                                                     │
│  Volume in drive F is Data                                                     │
│  Volume Serial Number is                                                       │
│                                                                                │
│  Directory of F:\cpp                                                           │
│                                                                                │
│ 24-05-2018  12:20    <DIR>          .                                          │
│ 24-05-2018  12:20    <DIR>          ..                                         │
│ 24-05-2018  11:57               130 helloworld.cpp                             │
│ 24-05-2018  12:19         1,564,138 helloworld.exe                            │
│                2 File(s)      1,564,268 bytes                                  │
│                2 Dir(s)  178,231,631,872 bytes free                            │
│                                                                                │
│ F:\cpp>                                                                      ∨ │
└────────────────────────────────────────────────────────────────────────────────┘
```

As seen, *helloworld.exe* has been created. To execute, just type *helloworld.exe* and hit Enter. The output should look like this:

```
┌─────────────────────────────────────────────────── CMD ─────────────── _ □ ✕ ─┐
│ F:\cpp>helloworld.exe                                                        ^ │
│ Hello World!!!                                                                 │
│                                                                                │
│ F:\cpp>                                                                        │
│                                                                                │
│                                                                              ∨ │
└────────────────────────────────────────────────────────────────────────────────┘
```

This is the compilation and execution procedure that will be followed thorough the course of this book.

If you are using GCC compiler on Linux/MAC, the same command:

```
$> g++ helloworld.cpp -o helloworld
```

Should compile the **helloworld.cpp** program and will create an executable file called **helloworld** (and not **helloworld.exe** as in Windows). To execute this file, use the following command:

```
$> ./helloworld
```

The following screenshot explains compilation (using g++) and execution procedure on Linux and MAC:

If you are using Clang compiler on Linux/MAC, use the following commad:

```
$> clang++ helloworld.cpp -o helloworld
```

This command will compile ***helloworld.cpp*** and generate an executable file ***helloworld***. To execute this file, use the following command:

```
$> ./helloworld
```

The following screenshot explains compilation (using clang++) and execution procedure on Linux and MAC:

Whichever operating system you may be using, you must have realized that the compilation and execution procedure remains more or less the same. In the following sections of the book we will learn several C++ concepts and compile and execute many C++ programs. Whichever OS/Text Editor/Compiler you choose, you should be very comfortable when it comes to compiling a program and then executing it.

3. Syntax

C++ is a case sensitive language. This means, "ebook" and "eBook" are treated differently. In this section, we will discuss the basic syntax of C++ and also learn to write a basic program.

3.1 Statements

A statement in a programming language carries out some computational function. Statements in C++ end with a semi-colon (;) . Although it is possible to have as many statements as desired on one line with each statement being separated with a semi-colon, it is not really recommended as the code will look messy and the code-readability will reduce. It is best practice to have one statement on one line. Some examples of statements are:

```
c = 50;
cout<< "Hello World";
int a = c * 2;
```

3.2 Blocks

A block is a group of statements enclosed within curly brackets ({ }). Here is an example:

```
{
    int a, b, c;
    cout<<"This is a block";
}
```

The usage of blocks is significant while working with decision making, loops, functions and classes. We will cover each of these in detail in the sections to follow.

3.3 Pre-processor directives

Pre-processor directives are statements that begin with a *hash* *(#)* symbol. Unlike normal statements, these ***do not*** end with a semi-colon and hence each pre-processor directive must be written on a new line. Pre-processor directives are processed before the compilation process begins. In a way, these provide meta information to the compiler. Here are some examples of pre-processor directives:

```
#include <iostream>
#define PI 3.14
#pragma startup myfunction
```

Pre-processor directives other than *#include* and *#define* are for advanced programmers, this book covers only the ones required.

3.4 Comments

Comments are ignored by the compiler and will not have any effect on the outcome of the compilation process. Usually, comments are explanatory statements but you can use them for any annotation purpose. C++ offers single-line and multi-line comments. Single line comments start with double-slash (//) and must terminate on the same line. Multi line comments are like a block of comments and are enclosed within this character sequence – slash-asterisk (/*) and asterisk-slash (*/).

Single Line Comment Example:

```
//This is a comment
//This is another comment
```

As seen each comment on a new line must begin with a double-slash.

Multi Line Comment Example:

```
/*
Comment block begins here.
As many lines can be added within the block.
No need for double slash ( // )
*/
```

3.5 Identifiers

Identifiers are used to identify variables, functions, classes & objects, etc. Identifier names can contain alphabets (a-z, A-Z), numbers (0 – 9) and underscore (_) but cannot start with a number and cannot contain any other special character.

3.6 Keywords

Keywords in C++ are reserved words which cannot be used as identifier names. Keywords have a specific meaning which tells the compiler what to do. Here is a list of them in alphabetical order:

asm	else	new	this

auto	enum	operator	throw
bool	explicit	private	true
break	export	protected	try
case	extern	public	typedef
catch	false	register	typeid
char	float	reinterpret_cast	typename
class	for	return	union
const	friend	short	unsigned
const_cast	goto	signed	using
continue	if	sizeof	virtual
default	inline	static	void
delete	int	static_cast	volatile
do	long	struct	wchar_t
double	mutable	switch	while
dynamic_cast	namespace	template	

3.7 Basic C++ Program Structure

A very basic standalone C++ program must have the following constituents:

1. *#include <iostream>* Statement:

As discussed in **Section 3.3**, all statements that start with a hash (#) symbol are pre-processor directives. A *#include* directive instructs the compiler which **header** to include. A **header** contains the definitions of variables, functions and classes

& objects which can be used for various purposes. General syntax to include a header is as follows:

```
#include <header here>
Eg:
#include <iostream>
#include <fstream>
```

The **#include** statement can also be used to include header file, either provided by the compiler or user defined local ones (placed in the same directory as the program). To include a local header file, the file name must be placed inside double quotes and not inside pointed brackets as follows:

```
#include "my_header_file.h"
```

#include < iostream > Statements instructs the compiler to include the **iostream** header which provides an **Input/Output Stream** used to read data from the user and display data on the screen. If you want to write a standalone C++ program that interacts with the user either by accepting inputs or displaying something on the screen, you have to place **#include < iostream >** in your program, usually on the first few lines.

There are many such built-in headers provided by different compilers. For example, *fstream* header is used for File Input/Output, *iomanip* is used for formatting output to be displayed on the screen, *cmath* provides definitions to carry out mathematical functions and so on. C++ is also backward compatible with most of the conventional C header files (the ones that end with .h), for example – ***stdlib.h, stdio.h, math.h,*** *float.h*, etc. These are provided by the compiler software and hence these shall be placed inside pointed brackets and not quotes as follows:

```
#include <stdlib.h>
#include <float.h>
```

2. Main Method

Main method serves as an entry point of the program. Every standalone C++ program must have a main method else the program will not know where to start executing from. Main method is essentially a function block enclosed within curly brackets ({ }). The general syntax of a main method is as follows:

```
int main ( )
{
    Statements....
    return 0;
}
```

Combining what we have learned in this section, here is a C++ program that does not do anything but compiles and executes properly.

```
#include <iostream>
int main ( )
{
    //No meaningful statements, just a comment.
    return 0;
}
```

You may try compiling and executing the above program. The process will go ahead without a problem but you will not see anything meaningful on the screen as the program does not do anything. Here's what you will see after compilation and execution:

3.7.1 First C++ Program

Now, let us learn to write a simple C++ program which displays a message on the screen. The *iostream* header provides an object called *cout* which is used to display data on the *standard character output* device, which in most cases is the computer screen. There is a way to redirect output to a different device using *I/O streams* and not the default computer screen, which is fairly an advanced topic and beyond the scope of this book. You will invariably use *cout* to display data only on the screen throughout the course of this book. *cout* belongs to the *std* namespace of the *iostream* header and hence *std ::* needs to be prefixed to *cout*.

The general syntax of using *cout* is:

```
std :: cout << [data];
```

cout is followed by an ***insertion operator (< <)*** which is followed by some data to be displayed. This data can be a constant, an expression or a variable. To display a message, a constant string can be used enclosed in double quotes. For example:

```
std :: cout << "This is a test message";
```

You can display as many expressions as you want with a new insertion operator:

```
std :: cout << "This is message 1 " << " This is message 2" ;
```

To insert a new line on the screen ***endl*** is used which belongs to the ***std*** namespace and hence ***std ::*** needs to be prefixed. This is not a part of the string; hence it should be outside the quotes, but after a new insertion operator:

```
std :: cout << "This is line 1" << std :: endl << "This is line 2" << std :: endl ;
```

Now that we have learned about the basic program structure and how to display a message on the screen, let us put together all the concepts and write a C++ program to display some text on the screen. If you have understood the covered chapters so far, you will not have a problem in understanding the following code:

```
//Include the iostream header
```

```
#include <iostream>
//Mandatory main method
int main ()
{
    /*
    Display some text on the screen using std :: cout
    Used std :: endl for inserting a new line
    */
    std :: cout << std :: endl << "This is my first
    C++ program.";
    std :: cout << std :: endl << "Let's say Hello
    World!!!";
    std :: cout << std :: endl << "Another Message on
    a new line.";
    std :: cout << std :: endl ;
//Mandatory return statement
return 0;
}
```

The output of this program should look like this:

Prefixing *std ::* to *cout*, *endl* and other members of the *std* namespace may be cumbersome. There is a way to avoid this by telling the compiler in the beginning that you will be using the *std namespace*. This is done with the help of the *using* keyword; the following statement should be inserted after the include statement:

```
using namespace std;
```

If you have included this statement in your code, *std :: cout* becomes *cout*, *std :: endl* becomes *endl* and all the other members of the *std namespace* can be used without *std ::* .

Instead of *endl*, the escape sequence '*\n*' can be used <u>within a string</u> to insert a new line. Another useful escape sequence is '*\t*' which is used to insert a tab-space.

Let us write another C++ program by including the *using namespace std* statement in order to get rid of the *std ::* prefix. The program shall also demonstrate the usage '\n' and '\t' escape sequences:

```
//Include the iostream header
#include <iostream>

//Statement to get rid of std :: prefix
using namespace std;

//Mandatory main method
int main ()
{
    /*
    Display some text on the screen using cout
    Used endl and "\n" for inserting a new line
    Also used "\t" escape sequence
```

```
*/
cout << "\nThis is my second C++ program.";
cout << endl << "\tLeaving 1 tab-space indent";
cout << endl << "\tThis line demonstrate the
proper use of horizontal tab.";
cout << endl ;

//Mandatory return statement
return 0;

}
```

The output of the above program should look like this:

It is worth noting how clean the code looks without the *std ::* prefix after including *the using namespace std* statement. All our subsequent programs should carry this statement.

3.8 Compilation Error

If you do not follow the C++ syntax and rules, you will run into compilation errors. Sometimes, the compiler will tell you where you have gone wrong, sometimes it will not and the error message will be generic in nature. It is important to keep a close eye on the code that you write and follow the syntax strictly.

Let us take an example where we will not follow the syntax on purpose for the sake of demonstrating compilation errors. Here is a code where I do not end a *cout* statement with a semicolon:

```cpp
#include <iostream>

using namespace std;

int main ()
{
    //cout statement without a semicolon
    //This should raise an error during compilation
    cout << "Hello World!!!"
    return 0;
}
```

This is what happens during compilation:

In this case, the error message is quite accurate and tells you what exactly has gone wrong. The compilation process was not successful and hence no output file would be generated. This is confirmed by the *dir* command which lists all the files present in the current directory:

```
F:\cpp\test>dir
 Volume in drive F is Data
 Volume Serial Number is

 Directory of F:\cpp\test

26-05-2018  09:15    <DIR>          .
26-05-2018  09:15    <DIR>          ..
26-05-2018  09:16               193 errordemo.cpp
               1 File(s)            193 bytes
               2 Dir(s)  178,214,232,064 bytes free

F:\cpp\test>_
```

4. Data Types

A data type is used to define the type of data we are dealing with. While programming, we use various variables to store data. When a variable is declared, it is allotted some memory in the memory location. Based on the type of data used, appropriate memory is allocated. C++ offers built-in data types as well as user-defined ones. User defined data types are formed using classes and objects. If you are familiar with programming, you must have already heard of data types such as *int* (for integer values), *float* (for floating point/decimal values), *char* (for character values), etc. Here's a list of built in data types:

Type	Size	Range
char	1 byte	-127 to 127 or 0 to 255
unsigned char	1 byte	0 to 255
signed char	1 byte	-127 to 127
int	4 bytes	-2147483648 to 2147483647
unsigned int	4 bytes	0 to 4294967295
signed int	4 bytes	-2147483648 to 2147483647
short int	2 bytes	-32768 to 32767
unsigned short int	2 bytes	0 to 65,535
signed short int	2 bytes	-32768 to 32767
long int	4 bytes	-2,147,483,648 to 2,147,483,647
signed long int	4 bytes	-2,147,483,648 to 2,147,483,647
unsigned long int	4 bytes	0 to 4,294,967,295
float	4 bytes	-1.17549e-38 to -3.40282e+38
double	8 bytes	-2.22507e-308 to -1.79769e+308)

long double	12 bytes	Variable across OS

These are the built-in primitive data types. As seen, there is no mention of a string data type. This is because, a string is just a sequence of characters and an array of characters works well as a string. However, C++ offers a separate non-primitive data type called *string class* which is a part of the *std namespace.*

<u>Note:</u> While the Size and Range values are the same as mentioned above most of the times, but may vary from compiler to compiler and/or OS to OS. This is not much of a problem unless you write low-level performance critical applications in a constrained environment such as embedded systems.

Fun Exercise

To show the size variation of data types across different operating systems, here is a fun exercise – there is an operator called *sizeof( )* which returns the size of the mentioned data, data type, variable or constant. The following code was compiled and executed on Windows and Linux OS separately using GCC:

```cpp
#include <iostream>
using namespace std;
int main()
{
    cout << "\nSize of int: " << sizeof(int) << endl
    ;
    cout << "Size of long int: " << sizeof(long int)
    << endl ;
    cout << "Size of char: " << sizeof(char) << endl
    ;
    cout << "Size of float: " << sizeof(float) <<
    endl ;
    cout << "Size of long double: " << sizeof(long
    double) << endl ;
```

```
    return 0;
}
```

Sizes of some data types were different on Windows and Linux.

Windows Output:

Linux Output:

5. Variables and Constants

5.1 Variables

A variable is a name given to a memory location which holds data. When a variable is declared, some space needs to be reserved in the system memory. This is done by the operating system. The memory allocation is usually random in nature and hence variable names come in handy as aliases to memory locations. In the previous section, we have learned about the available built-in data types in C++. A data type must be specified while declaring a variable. General Syntax:

```
<data type> <variable name>;
eg:
int a;
float b;
char c;
string name;
```

Variables of the same data type can be declared on the same line by separating them using a comma:

```
<data type> <variable 1>, <variable 2>;
eg:
int a, b, c;
float x, y;
long double m, n;
```

It is also possible to initialize variables by assigning them a value using the assignment operator (=). There is a chapter in this book which explains operators in depth. As of now, you only have to understand how the assignment operator works. The job of the assignment operator is to assign the value of the right operand to the left operand. For example:

```
int a = 20, b, c = 355;
float x = 2.45;
char z = 'c';
string word = "eBook"
```

5.2 Constants

Constants are read-only values which cannot be changed in the program later. In *Section 3.7.1*, we have learned to write basic C++ programs where we used *cout* to display messages on the screen. The message was essentially a *constant string expression*. We will learn more about strings in the *Strings* chapter of this book.

There are two ways to define constants. The first one involves using the *const* keyword and the second one using the *#define* pre-processor directive.

5.2.1 const Keyword

A variable can be defined as a constant by prefixing the *const* keyword at the time of declaration. Because you cannot change the value of a constant, it is important to initialize the variable at the time of declaration. The general syntax is as follows:

```
const <data type> <variable name> = <value>;
eg:
const int num = 100;
const float x = 1.25;
//All variables will become constants:
const char first = 'c', last = 'b';
```

```
const string country = "USA";
```

5.2.2 #define Pre-processor directive

All pre-processor directives are read and interpreted before the compilation process begins. ***#define*** directive is used to define custom identifiers and set their values. Since this process happens before the actual compilation, these custom identifiers are not treated as traditional variable. These statements do not terminate with a semicolon. General Syntax:

#define <identifier> <value>
eg:
#define number 123
#define name "Chad"
#define PI 3.14

As seen, there is no need to specify a data type and you can define all sorts of constant identifiers with the ***#define*** directive. The way this method works is slightly different. When the compiler encounters a ***#define*** directive, the subsequent identifier and its corresponding value is fetched. The compiler then directly substitutes this identifier with its fetched value wherever that particular identifiers appears in the code. This is a part of the pre-processing step and is transparent to the user; meaning, the user does not see this happening.

This method will get clearer with an example. Let us consider there are two identifiers called – ***shape*** and ***PI*** having values of ***"Circle"*** and ***3.14*** respectively. Here is a code snippet:

```
#define shape "Circle"
#define PI 3.14
using namespace std;
int main ( )
{
    cout << shape << endl << PI << endl;
    return 0;
}
```

When this code is sent for compilation, during pre-processing the values of *shape* and *PI* will be substituted wherever *shape* and *PI* appear in the code. After pre-processing, the above code will look like the following to the compiler (and not the user):

```
using namespace std;
int main ( )
{
    cout << "Circle" << endl << 3.14 << endl;
    return 0;
}
```

Here is a well commented C++ program that demonstrates the usage of variables and constants:

```
#include <iostream>
//Define constants using #define
#define PI 3.14
#define country "USA"

using namespace std;

int main ()
{
    //Declare integer variables, initialize some
    int number = 587, x, y;
    //Declare integer variables, initialize some
    float a = 14.65, b = 60.78;
    //Declare constant character variables
    const char first = 'c', last = 'b';
```

```
//Declare string values
string word = "eBook";
//Display all variables/constants using cout
//A cout statement can span across multiple lines
cout  <<  endl  <<  endl  <<  "Displaying
variables:\n\n"
<< "number: " << number << endl
<< "a: " << a << endl
<< "b: " << b << endl
<< "first: " << first << endl
<< "last: " << last << endl
<< "word: " << word << endl ;
//Display constants defined using #define
cout << endl << "Displaying identifiers defined
using #define:\n\n"
<< "PI: " << PI << endl
<< "country: " << country << endl << endl ;

return 0;
}
```

Output:

___Note:___ While assigning values to variables, the data type of the variable must be considered. A variable can hold data of its type only. For example, an integer variable **cannot hold** a string value. This will cause a data type mismatch situation as shown below:

```
int x = "Hello!!!"; //This is unacceptable, only for
demonstration
```

Some assignment between similar data types is fine. For example, you can assign a float value to an integer variable but it will lose precision. That is, if you try to assign *5.6* to an *integer variable*, only *5* will be stored as an integer and the decimal part will be discarded.

5.3 Scope of a Variable

The usage of a variable is restricted to the block in which it is defined. A variable that is defined outside all blocks, including outside all functions and main function is called a *global variable*. Such a variable can be accessed from any block and has a default value of 0 in case of integers and floats. A global variable should be accessed with the help of a scope resolution operator (::) . The general syntax is explained in the following snippet:

```
int number = 75;
int main ( )
{
    int number = 50;
    cout << "Global: " << :: number << endl
    << "Local: " << number << endl;
    return 0;
}
```

The statement *:: number* will access the *global variable* number which has a value of *75*. Whereas the statement *number* will access the *local variable* number from inside the *main method* which has the value of *50*.

6. User Interaction

In the previous sections we have seen how *cout* is used to display data on the screen. In this section, we will see how to interact with the user, how to accept inputs from the user.

The *iostream* header provides an object called *cin* which is used to accept input from the user. *cin* just as *cout* is a member of the *std namespace*. Usage is slightly different, the *cin* object should be followed by the *extraction operator (>>)* and a variable. General Syntax:

```
cin >> [variable];
eg:
string name;
cin >> name;
```

The usage of *cin* is a <u>blocking I/O operation</u>. That is, when a *cin* statement is encountered, the program will halt the execution and wait for the user to enter something through the keyboard. In the above example, when the execution control reaches *cin >> name;* statement, the program will wait for the user to enter some text. Once the user does so and hits Enter, whatever the user has entered will be extracted and stored in the variable *name*. You can read multiple values into multiple variables by using the *extraction operator (>>)* multiple times as follows:

```
cin >> [variable 1] >> [variable 2] >> …. >>
[variable n];
eg:
cin >> first_name >> last_name ;
```

The number of variable you try to read is the number of times the program will wait for the user to enter some data. The entered data will be fetched in the order of the specified variables. Here is a simple well commented C++ program that prompts the user to enter several values and then displays them:

```cpp
#include <iostream>

using namespace std;

int main ()
{
    //Declare variables to store user input
    string first_name, last_name, address;
    int age;
    double weight;

    //Ask the user to enter first and last name
    cout << endl << endl
    << "Enter First and Last Name: " << endl ;
    //Read two inputs into first_name and last_name
    cin >> first_name >> last_name ;

    //Ask the user to enter address
    //cin >> is not capable of reading strings with
    space
    //getline function is used to read proper strings
    //which is discussed later in this book
    cout << endl << endl
    << "Enter address: " << endl;
    cin >> address;

    //Ask the user to enter age and weight
    cout << endl << endl
    << "Enter age and weight: " << endl ;
    cin >> age >> weight ;

    //Display all the input values
    cout << endl << endl
    << "First Name: " << first_name << endl
    << "Last Name: " << last_name << endl
    << "Address: " << address << endl
    << "Age: " << age << endl
    << "Weight: " << weight << endl ;
```

```
    return 0;

}
```

Output:

```
                            CMD                    _ □ ×
F:\cpp>g++ userinput.cpp -o userinput

F:\cpp>userinput.exe

Enter First and Last Name:
Matthew
Johnson

Enter address:
Ottawa

Enter age and weight:
25
63.2

First Name: Matthew
Last Name: Johnson
Address: Ottawa
Age: 25
Weight: 63.2

F:\cpp>_
```

Note: The **_cin >>_** statement can read all primitive data types without a problem. It can also read strings in some cases. However, it cannot be used to read strings with spaces. If a string with spaces is entered, each value after the space is going to be treated as a new input and each new input will go to the next variable if available. If no more variables are present, those values after the space will be just discarded. This shortfall of **_cin >>_** statement can lead to data type mismatch and can cause to program to behave differently. Let us execute the same program and demonstrate.

Instead of entering **_Matthew (first_name)_** and **_Johnson (last_name)_** as two different inputs, I will place them on a single

45

line separated by a space. The output shows that the program behaves totally fine and **Matthew** and **Johnson** are fetched as *first_name* and *last_name* correctly:

Now, let us do another run and try to introduce a space in the *address* variable. Instead of **Ottawa**, let us enter **New York**. Theoretically, *"New"* should go to the *address* variable and *"York"* will be treated as another input as there is a space after *"New"*. After reading address, we ask the user to enter age and weight. The program will try to extract *"York"* in the *age* variable which is of *integer* type. This is will lead to a data mismatch situation and will cause the program to lose stability. Here is the output:

As seen, the program behaves as expected in an unstable manner. We will discuss the correct way of reading strings even with spaces using the **getline** function in the **Strings** section of this book.

7. Operators

An operator in a programming language is a symbol that performs a specific task. Operators in C++ are used to perform mathematical, logical or comparison operations. The following types of operators are available:

1. Arithmetic Operators

2. Logical Operators

3. Bitwise Operators

4. Relational Operators

5. Assignment Operators

7.1 Arithmetic Operators

Arithmetic operators are used to perform arithmetic/ mathematical operations such as addition, subtraction, division, etc.

Operator	Description	Sample Usage	Explanation
+	Addition	a + b	Performs arithmetic addition, returns sum of the operands.
-	Subtraction	a - b	Performs arithmetic subtraction, returns difference of the operands.
*	Multiplication	a * b	Multiplies operands and returns the arithmetic product.
/	Division	a / b	Performs division and returns the arithmetic quotient.
%	Modulus	a % b	Performs division and returns the remainder. Usage is restricted to integer type operands only.
++	Increment	a ++	Increments the value of an operand by 1. Two variations: Post increment (a ++) and Pre increment (++ a). This operator works only on integer variables.
--	Decrement	a --	Decrements the value of an operand by 1. Two variations: Post increment (a --) and Pre increment (-- a). This operator works only on integer variables.

Note: Integer by Integer division will result in the quotient being an integer even if the arithmetic value of the quotient should be false. For example, the quotient resulting from this division – *5 / 2* will be *2* and not *2.5*. To solve this, a float factor must be introduced. You can multiply 1.0 to either the numerator or the denominator. The expression *5 / 2* will now become *5 * 1.0 / 2* or *5 / 2 * 1.0*. You can even use brackets just as you would in mathematics for convenience or when you want to carry out an operation first among an expression – *5 / (2 * 1.0)*.

eg:
int x = 15, y = 4;
float quotient = (x * 1.0) / y;

7.2 Logical Operators

Logical operators are used to carry out logical AND, OR and NOT. These return 0 or 1. 0 (and negative numbers) is regarded as false and 1 (and all positive numbers) is regarded as true.

Operator	Description	Sample Usage	Explanation
&&	Logical AND	a && b	Compares operands and returns 1 if all the values are non-zero, returns 0 otherwise.
||	Logical OR	a || b	Compares operands and returns 1 if any one of the values is non-zero, returns 0 if .
!	Logical NOT	!a	Returns inverted value of the operand. If the operand has a true value (non-zero), 0 will be returned and if the operand has false value (0 or negative), 1 will be returned.

7.3 Bitwise Operators

Bitwise operators are used to perform bit-by-bit logical operation. That is, operations are carried out on each bit of the operands.

Operator	Description	Sample Usage	Explanation
&	Bitwise Logical AND	a & b	Performs logical AND on each of the operands on a bit-by-bit basis.
|	Bitwise Logical OR	a | b	Performs logical OR on each of the operands on a bit-by-bit basis.
~	Bitwise Logical Inverter	~a	Inverts each bit of the operand.
^	Bitwise Logical XOR	a ^ b	Performs logical XOR on each of the operands on a bit-by-bit basis.
<<	Left Shift	a << b	Left shifts bits of the operand on the left by a number specified by the right operand. From *Sample Usage*, *a << b* will result in a's bits left shifted b times.
>>	Right Shift	a >> b	Right shifts bits of the operand on the left by a number specified by the right operand. From *Sample Usage*, *a >> b* will result in a's bits right shifted b times.

7.4 Relational Operators

Relational Operators are used to compare the given operands. These operators return either 0 (false) or 1 (true).

Operator	Description	Sample Usage	Explanation
==	Equal To	a == b	Returns 1 if the value of the operands is equal, 0 otherwise.
!=	Not Equal To	a != b	Returns 1 if the value of the operands is not equal, 0 otherwise.
<	Less Than	a < b	Returns 1 if the value of the left operand is less than the value of the operand on the right, 0 otherwise.
>	Greater Than	a > b	Returns 1 if the value of the left operand is greater than the value of the operand on the right, 0 otherwise.
<=	Less Than OR Equal To	a <= b	Returns 1 if the value of the left operand is less than OR equal to the value of the operand on the right, 0 otherwise.
>=	Greater Than OR Equal To	a >= b	Returns 1 if the value of the left operand is greater than OR equal to the value of the operand on the right, 0 otherwise.

7.5 Assignment Operators

The equal-to (=) sign is the assignment operator in C++ and many other programming languages. It is used to assign values to variables. We have seen the basic usage of the assignment operator in *Section 5*. In this section, we will discuss assignment operators in detail. General Syntax:

```
<operand 1> = <operand 2>
eg:
a = 70;
b = a * 2;
c = b;
```

Assignment operator, assigns the value of the operand on the right to the operand on the left. Operand on the left side of the assignment operator has to be a variable. Operand on the right side of the assignment operator can be a constant, variable or an expression. In case of an expression, it will be evaluated first and then the value will be assigned except when a post-increment operator is used as demonstrated in the code snippet below:

```
int a, b, c = 100 ;
a = c * 100 ;
b = c ++;
```

Before assigning a value to variable a, the expression $c * 100$ will be evaluated first. Hence the variable a will now hold a value of 10000. Whereas, the value of c will be assigned to variable b first and then c will be incremented. Hence variable b will now hold 100 and variable c will now hold 100. If you want to increment first and then assign, pre-increment operator needs to be used: $b = ++c$.

7.5.1 Compound Assignment Operators

Compound Assignment Operators are used to perform mathematical operations on operands first and then assign.

Operator	Description	Sample Usage	Equivalent To
+=	Perform arithmetic addition, then assign	a += b	a = a + b
-=	Perform arithmetic subtraction, then assign	a -= b	a = a - b
*=	Perform arithmetic multiplication, then assign	a *= b	a = a * b
/=	Perform arithmetic division, then assign	a /= b	a = a / b
%=	Calculate modulus, then assign	a %= b	a = a % b
&=	Perform Bitwise Logical AND, then assign	a &= b	a = a & b
|=	Perform Bitwise Logical OR, then assign	a |= b	a = a | b
^=	Perform Bitwise Logical XOR, then assign	a ^= b	a = a ^ b
<<=	Perform left shift, then assign	a <<= b	a = a << b
>>=	Perform right shift, then assign	a >>= b	a = a >> b

To understand the working of bitwise operators, some knowledge of **Boolean Algebra** and **Binary Number System** is needed. For now, let us see how to represent an integer in a binary form. The **bitset** header provides an object called **bitset** (part of **std namespace)** which is used to work with binary representations. Usage of **bitset** will need **#include <bitset>** in your program. Syntax for representing an integer in binary form:

```
bitset<number of bits>
(variable/constant/expression)
eg:
int a = 4;
```

```
cout << bitset<8> (a);
```

If you convert **4** from **_decimal number system_** to **_binary number system_**, you will get a binary value of **_100_**. **_8-bit_** binary representation of **4** is – **_0000 0100_**. In the above example, **_00000100_** will be displayed on the screen.

Let us write a simple program that accepts two integer values from the user and demonstrates the usage of some of the operators. Logical and Relational Operators are best understood in conjunction with **_Control Structures_**, hence their usage is demonstrated in the next section (**_Section 8_**).

Go through the comments in the following code in order to understand it better:

```cpp
#include <iostream>
#include <bitset> //Needed for using bitset<8>

using namespace std;

int main ()
{
    //Declare the variables that we need
    int x, y, sum, difference, product, modulus;
    //Declare a float var to store quotient
    float quotient;
    //Ask the user to enter two values
    cout << endl << endl
    << "Enter two integers: " << endl ;
    //Read two inputs
    cin >> x >> y;
    //Display entered valued in decimal and binary
    cout << endl
        << "x: " << x << endl
        << "y: " << y << endl
        << "x (8-bit binary): " << bitset<8> (x) <<
        endl
```

```cpp
        << "y (8-bit binary): " << bitset<8> (y) <<
        endl;
//Calculate  sum,  difference,  product,  quotient
and modulus
sum = x + y ;
difference = x - y ;
product = x * y ;
quotient = x / ( y * 1.0) ;
modulus = x % y ;
//Display claculated values
cout << endl
        << "x + y : " << sum << endl
        << "x - y : " << difference << endl
        << "x * y : " << product << endl
        << "x / y : " << quotient << endl
        << "x % y : " << modulus << endl;
//Perform Bitwise Operations and display directly
cout << endl
        << "x & y : " << bitset<8> (x & y) << endl
        << "x | y : " << bitset<8> (x | y) << endl
        << "~x : " << bitset<8> (~x) << endl
        << "~y : " << bitset<8> (~y) << endl
        << "x ^ y : " << bitset<8> (x ^ y) << endl
        << "x << y : " << bitset<8> (x << y) << endl
        << "x >> y : " << bitset<8> (x >> y) << endl ;

    return 0;
}
```

Output:

```
F:\cpp>g++ operatorsdemo.cpp -o operatorsdemo

F:\cpp>operatorsdemo.exe

Enter two integers:
125
3

x: 125
y: 3
x (8-bit binary): 01111101
y (8-bit binary): 00000011

x + y : 128
x - y : 122
x * y : 375
x / y : 41.6667
x % y : 2

x & y : 00000001
x | y : 01111111
~x : 10000010
~y : 11111100
x ^ y : 01111110
x << y : 11101000
x >> y : 00001111

F:\cpp>_
```

8. Control Structures

Control Structures are used to exercise control over the execution of the program. C++ offers control structures in the form of decision making constructs (if-else and switch) and loops.

8.1 Decision Making

Decision making constructs are available in the form of if-else statements and switch-case statements.

8.1.1 if-else Construct

The general syntax for using an if statement is as follows:

```
if ( <condition> )
{
   //This is the if-block
   <statements...>
}
```

Once the execution control reaches the *if* statement, the expression in the *<condition>* field is evaluated. The *<condition>* is treated as a Boolean expression. Evaluation of this expression can either evaluate to 0 (false) or 1 (true). If the evaluation of the Boolean expression returns *1*, the statements inside the *if-block* are executed, a *0* value will skip the execution of the *if-block*. A block is enclosed within curly brackets ({ }). The *if-block* can be followed by an optional *else-block* as follows:

```
if ( <condition> )
{
   //This is the if-block
   <statements...>
}
   else
{
   //This is the else-block
   <statements...>
}
```

When there are *if* and *else* blocks and the specified condition of the *if statement* evaluates to *false*, only then the *else-block* will be executed.

Note: The *else block* should immediately follow the *if block* which means there can be no statements after the end of the *if block* and just before the else statement.

It is also possible to nest if-else statements as follows:

```
if ( <condition 1>)
{
   //This block will be executed if <condition 1> is
   true.
   if ( <condition 2> )
   {
      //This block will be executed if <condition 1>
      and <condition 2> is true.
      <statements...>
   }
   else
   {
      //This block will be executed if <condition 1>
      is true and <condition 2> is false.
```

```
        <statements...>
    }
  }
  else
{
    //This block will be executed if <condition 1> is
    false.
    if ( <condition 3> )
    {
        //This block will be executed if <condition 1>
        is false and <condition 3> is true.
        <statements...>
    }
}
```

There is another way of writing **if-else** decision making construct using the **else if** statement. The way **else if** construct work is – There will be a mandatory **if** statement, if the condition of the **if** statement evaluates to **false**, the control will go to the immediate **else if** statement (if it is present) and will evaluate the condition of the **else if** statement. If it evaluates to **1**, the **else if** block will be executed and the remaining **else if** and **else blocks** (if present) will be ignored; if it evaluates to **0**, the control will go to the next **else if** or **else** statements if there are any. You can have as many **else if** statements as you want. The general syntax is as follows:

```
if ( <condition 1>)
{
    //This block will be executed if <condition 1> is
    true.
}
else if ( <condition 2> )
```

```
{
    //This block will be executed if <condition 1> is
    false <condition 2> is true.
    <statements...>
}
else if ( <condition 3> )
{
    //This block will be executed if <condition 1>
    and <condition 2> are false and <condition 3> is
    true.
    <statements...>
}
else
{
    //This block will be executed if <condition 1>,
    <condition 2> and <condition 3> are false.
}
```

Note: If there is only one statement inside an if, else if or else block, there is no need to specify the block inside curly brackets.

Here is a simple C++ program that demonstrates the usage of if-else statements. The program accepts an integer from the user and checks if it is positive, negative or zero:

```
#include <iostream>

using namespace std;

int main ()
{
    //Declare an integer to accept and store user
    input
    int number;
    //Ask the user to enter a number
    cout << endl << endl
    << "Enter a number: " ;
    //Wait for user input, accept it into number var
    cin >> number;
```

```
//Check if positive, negative or zero
//Check if greater than 0, meaning positive:
if ( number > 0 )
cout << "The number: " << number << " is
Positive." << endl;
//Check if less than 0, meaning positive:
else if ( number < 0 )
cout << "The number: " << number << " is
Negative." << endl;
//If the number is neither positive, nor
negative, it is Zero
else
cout << "The number: " << number << " is Zero."
<< endl;
return 0;
}
```

The program has been executed 3 times to demonstrate each case. Here is the output:

8.1.2 switch-case Construct

There can arise a time where a situation can lead to multiple possibilities. In programmatic terms, evaluation of an expression can lead to more than one outcomes. Sure you can have a long list of *if*, *else if* and nested *if* statements to address such a situation; it will work perfectly fine. But there is a cleaner, efficient and more organized way to do this using the *switch-case* construct. The general syntax of a *switch-case* construct is:

```
switch (<expression>)
{
    case <constant expression 1>:
        //Statements to be executed if this case is
        matched.
    case <constant expression 1>:
        //Statements to be executed if this case is
        matched.
    ... ...

    ... ...

    ... ...

    case <constant expression N>:
        //Statements to be executed if this case is
        matched.
    default:
        //Statements to be executed if no case is
        matched.
}
```

A switch statement must be supplied with an expression which is evaluated and a decision is made. The supplied expression is denoted by *< expression >* field in the above code snippet. Each outcome that this expression can evaluate to is known as a *case*. When the *< expression >* is evaluated, the program looks for the matching constant expression supplied with each of the cases present inside the switch block. If a match is found, that particular *case block* is executed. If no match is found, the program executes the *default case* block if present. This process is known as *testing for cases*. An important thing to note here is – once a matching case is found, all the statements after that case block are executed until a **break;** statement is encountered. A **break;** statement is used to take the control out of a switch block. It is also possible to nest switch blocks. In case of nested switch blocks, a break statement encountered in the inner switch block will only bring the control out of that particular block and not from the whole nested switch arrangement.

Let us write a program that will ask the user to enter an integer and check if it odd or even. To do so, we divide the given number by 2 and check its remainder. That is, we perform **< number > % 2** operation to get the remainder:

```cpp
#include <iostream>

using namespace std;

int main ()
{
    //Declare a variable to store user input
    int number;
    //Ask the user to enter a number
    cout << endl << endl
    << "Enter a positive integer: ";
    //Wait for the user to enter
    cin >> number;
    //Check for odd even using switch
    switch ( number % 2)
    {
        //If number % 2 is 0, then even
        case 0:
            cout << "The number: " << number << " is
            EVEN." ;
            break;
        //If number % 2 is 1, then even
        case 1:
            cout << "The number: " << number << " is
            ODD.";
            break;
```

```
//Default case for any other outcome.
//For example, -1 as input.
default:
      cout << "The number: " << number << " is an
      invalid input.";
}
cout << endl ;

return 0;

}
```

The program was run 3 times to demonstrate different cases:

```
F:\cpp>switchdemo1.exe

Enter a positive integer: 42
The number: 42 is EVEN.
F:\cpp>switchdemo1.exe

Enter a positive integer: 653
The number: 653 is ODD.
F:\cpp>switchdemo1.exe

Enter a positive integer: -1
The number: -1 is an invalid input.
F:\cpp>
```

Let us take another example that demonstrates what happens
in the presence and in the absence of a *break;* statement in a
better way. Here is a C++ program to check whether an entered
character is a vowel or consonant:

```
#include <iostream>

using namespace std;

int main ()
{
```

```cpp
//Declare a variable to store user input
char input;
//Ask the user to enter a character
cout << endl << endl
<< "Enter a character: ";
//Wait for the user to enter
cin >> input;
//Check for vowel or consonant
switch ( input )
{
    //Cases for vowels
    case 'a':
    case 'e':
    case 'i':
    case 'o':
    case 'u':
    case 'A':
    case 'E':
    case 'I':
    case 'O':
    case 'U':
        cout << "The entered char: " << input << "
        is a vowel." << endl;
        //Break the execution from case 'a' to case
        'U'
        break;
    //Default case for consonants
    default:
        cout << "The entered char: " << input << "
        is a consonant." << endl;
}
return 0;
}
```

As seen from the above code, there is no ***break*** statement from ***case 'a'*** to ***case 'U'***. That is because all the intermediate cases are vowels and we do not want to break the execution if a vowel is detected. If we had used a ***break*** statement after every vowel case, then we would have had a ***cout*** statement inside every vowel case to display that the input character is a vowel. Here is the output:

```
CMD                                    -  □  ×

F:\cpp>g++ vowelconsonant.cpp -o vowelconsonant

F:\cpp>vowelconsonant.exe

Enter a character: I
The entered char: I is a vowel.

F:\cpp>vowelconsonant.exe

Enter a character: e
The entered char: e is a vowel.

F:\cpp>vowelconsonant.exe

Enter a character: X
The entered char: X is a consoant.

F:\cpp>vowelconsonant.exe

Enter a character: u
The entered char: u is a vowel.

F:\cpp>
```

8.2 Loops

Loops are used to execute a group of statements over and over again until a specified condition is met. C++ offers 3 loops – *while loop, do while loop and for loop*. We will look at each one of these in detail.

8.2.1 while Loop

```
Syntax for using while loop is as follows:

while (<condition>)
{
    //Statements…
}
```

A while loop should be supplied with a condition denoted by the *< condition >* field in the above snippet. If the specified condition evaluates to *1 or a non-zero number*, it is considered as *true* and the statements inside the while block are executed one by one. Once the execution reaches the end of the block, the specified condition is checked again and if it evaluates to a non-zero number, the block is executed again. This process goes on until the specified condition evaluates to *0 or a negative number*. Each instance of a loop block execution is known as an *iteration*.

Here is a snippet to display numbers from 1 to 10 on the screen using a while loop:

```
//Initialize an integer variable to 1
int number = 1;
while ( number <= 10 )
{
    //Display number
    cout << number << " " ;
    //Increment number
    number ++;
}
```

8.2.2 do-while Loop

Syntax for using do-while loop is as follows:

```
do
{
    //Statements...
} while (<condition>);
```

The *do-while* loop works just like the *while* loop with one major difference. Instead of checking the specified condition at the beginning of the loop, it is checked at the end. That is, when the program encounters a do-while block, the statements inside it are immediately executed and then the condition is checked. This means, the statements under a *do-while* loop are guaranteed to

<u>be executed at least once</u> even if the specified condition evaluates to *0 or a negative number*.

Here is a snippet to display numbers from 1 to 10 on the screen using a do-while loop:

```
//Initialize an integer variable to 1
int number = 1;
do
{
    //Display number
    cout << number << " " ;
    //Increment number
    number ++;
} while ( number <= 10 );
```

8.3.3 for Loop

Syntax for using for loop is as follows:

```
for ( <loop variable initialization> ; <condition> ;
<expression> )
{
    <statements...>
}
```

The *for loop* has more features than the *while* and the *do while* loops. It allows you to use a special loop variable for iterating purpose. Until the specified *<condition>* evaluates to a non-zero number, the loop will go on executing. The *<expression>* can contain any mathematical expression, this field is usually used to increment or decrement the loop variable.

Here is a snippet to display numbers from 1 to 10 on the screen using a *for loop*:

```
//Declare an integer variable
int number;
for ( number = 1 ; number <= 10 ; number ++)
{
    //Display number
    cout << number << " " ;
}
```

It is also possible to nest loops. Let us write a C++ program to draw the following pattern using nested loops:

```
*

***

*****

*******

*********

***********

*************

***************

*****************

*******************
```

As seen, there are 10 lines in the pattern. Each line has odd number of stars (asterisks). The expression: *((2 x Line Number) – 1)* will give us the number of stars to be printed on each line.

We will need a total of 3 loops – one outer loop to keep track of the lines, two inner loops to keep track of the number of spaces to be left and the number of stars to be printed. Here is the code:

```cpp
#include <iostream>
using namespace std;
int main ()
{
    int i, j, k, space = 10, star = 0 ;
    cout << endl << endl ;
    //for loop for no. of lines
    for (i = 1 ; i <= 10 ; i ++)
    {
        space -- ;
        star = (2 * i) - 1;
        j = 0 ;
        //nested while loop for no. of spaces
        while ( j ++ < space )
        {
            //leave spaces "space" number of times
            cout << " ";
        }
        k = 0 ;
        //another while loop for no. of *
        while ( k ++ < star )
        {
            //print stars "star" number of times
            cout << "*";
        }
        cout << endl ;
    }
    cout << endl << endl ;
    return 0;
}
```

Output:

8.3.4 Control Statements

Control statements are used to exercise control over the execution of a loop. Normally, a loop would go on executing until the specified condition is met. Control statements allow you to control the execution of a loop beyond the specified condition. C++ offers two control statement – *break* and *continue*. We have already seen the usage of a *break* statement in *Section 8.2.1* to bring the control out of a *switch-case* block.

8.3.4.1 break Statement

A *break* statement is used to halt the execution of a loop. When a break statement is encountered, the execution control comes out of the loop block even if the specified condition evaluates to a non-zero number. Let us take an example. Consider you want to write a *while* loop to display integers from

1 to 10, but want to come out of the loop when the value reaches 7. Here is how that is done using break statement:

```
//Initialize a variable x to 1
int x = 1;
//Check if x is less than or equal to 10.
//As long as this condition is met, keep executing
the loop.
while ( x <= 10 )
{
    //When x becomes 7, break out of the loop.
    if ( x == 7 )
    break;
    //Write the value of x on the screen.
    cout << x << " ";
    //Increment x by 1.
    x++;
}
```

8.2.4.2 continue Statement

A *continue* statement is used to take the control to the starting of a loop. When a *continue* statement is encountered, the remaining statements in the loop block are ignored and the loop moves to the next iteration. In case of *while* and *do-while* loops, the control jumps back to the *while (<condition>)* and *do* statements respectively. In a *for* loop, a *continue* statement will take the execution control to the beginning of the loop there by incrementing/decrementing the loop variable. Consider you want to print only even values from 1 to 10. Here is how you can do it with a continue statement.

```
for ( int x = 1 ; x <= 10 ; x ++ )
```

```
{
    //If x is not divisible by 2, it means x is odd.
    //In such a case, you want to skip all the
    remaining statements.
    if ( x % 2 == 1 )
        continue;
    cout << x << " " ;
}
```

Note: If there is only one statement inside a loop block, no need to put it inside curly brackets.

Let us demonstrate the usage of control statements with the help of a programming tutorial. Here is a C++ program that accepts an integer from the user and checks if it is a prime or a composite number.

```
#include <iostream>

using namespace std;

int main ()
{
    //Declare an integer to accept and store user
    input
    //and also loop variable i
    int i, number;
    //Ask the user to enter a number
    cout << endl << endl
        << "Enter a number: " ;
    //Wait for user input, accept it into number var
    cin >> number;
    //Loop from 1 to number
    for ( i = 1 ; i <= number ; i ++)
    {
        //Skip when i is 1 as all numbers are
        divisible by 1
        if ( i == 1 )
        continue;
        //If number is divisible by i, break
        if ( number % i == 0 )
```

```cpp
        break;
    }
    //If the number is only divisible by itself
    if ( i == number )
        cout << endl << endl
            << "Number: " << number << " is prime." <<
            endl ;
        //If the number is divisible by some other
        number
        else
            cout << endl << endl
                << "Number: " << number << " is not
                prime." << endl ;
        return 0;
}
```

Output:

```
F:\cpp>g++ primeornot.cpp -o primeornot.exe

F:\cpp>primeornot.exe

Enter a number: 14

Number: 14 is not prime.
F:\cpp>primeornot.exe

Enter a number: 9

Number: 9 is not prime.
F:\cpp>primeornot.exe

Enter a number: 7

Number: 7 is prime.
F:\cpp>_
```

9. Functions

A function is a block of code that performs a specific task. Functions, synonymously called methods are used where a piece of code needs to be re-used. C++ standard library provides built-in functions and we can also define our own functions. There are two things to know when dealing with user defined functions – function definition and function call.

9.1 Function Definition

A function should be defined outside the main method. The general syntax is:

```
<return data type> <function name> ( <parameters> )
{
    //Function Body
    //Statements...
    return <value>; //Only if the function returns a
    value.
}
```

These are the important parts of a function definition – Return Data Type, Function Name, Parameters, Function Body.

Return Data Type

This field specifies the type of data the function returns. For example, if you have a function that returns the sum of two integers, the return type of that function will be *int*. If a function does not return any data, the return type should be *void*. If a function is returning a value, there has to be a mandatory return statement at the end of the function body.

Function Name

Function name is a name given to a function for identification purpose. This name is used to call the function.

Parameters

Parameters is a list of variables that a function accepts. These variables are sent to a function while calling the function. Each parameter is separated by a comma.

Function Body

This is the core part of function definition where the actual work of the function begins. This is where computational statements are placed. If a function returns a value, there has to be a mandatory return statement at the end of the function body. A function can only return one value.

Here are a few examples of function definitions:

A function that does not return any data, does not accept any parameters, only displays a message on the screen:

```
void display_message ( )
{
    cout << endl << "Hello! We are inside a function
    block! " << endl;
}
```

A function that accepts 3 parameters and displays their sum, does not return any data:

```
void display_sum (int x , int y , int z )
```

```
{
    cout << endl << "Sum: " << ( x + y + z ) << endl;
}
```

A function that accepts 2 integer values and returns the quotient of division in float form. The function should have float return type:

```
float divide ( int a, int b )
{
    float quotient = ( a * 1.0 ) / b;
    return quotient;
}
```

9.1.1 Function Prototyping

Function Prototyping is a process of declaring a function before defining it. This is always not mandatory but is a good programming practice. Function prototyping tells the compiler what kind of functions are present.

Syntax:

<return data type> <function name> (<parameters or parameter's type>);

Prototyping statement should be placed before the function definition, preferably on the first few lines, after **using namespace std;** statement. The prototype for the divide function from the previous example is as follows:

```
float divide ( int a, int b );
    { OR }
float divide ( int, int );
```

9.2 Function Call

A function definition contains a set of operation that a function performs. However, that code remains inactive unless a call is made to that function. Calling a function is also known as invoking a function. The general syntax is:

```
<function name> ( <parameters> );
```

Let us recall the definition of *display_sum* function explained as an example in *Section 9.1*:

```
void display_sum (int x , int y , int z )
{
    cout << endl << "Sum: " << ( x + y + z ) endl;
}
```

If we had to call this function, we would use the following statement:

```
display_sum ( 4, 5 , 10 );
```

The *display_sum* function accepts 3 integer values as parameters hence integer values of *4, 5 and 10* are passed as *function arguments* to it during the function call. These values will be received by x, y and z respectively.

If a function is returning a value, there should be a variable to receive that value. General Syntax:

```
<variable> = <function name> ( <parameters> );
```

If no variable is specified to receive returned value, the program will still be correct syntactically but the returned value will be lost.

Let us recall the definition of **divide** function explained as an example in **Section 9.1**:

```
float divide ( int a, int b )
{
    float quotient = ( a * 1.0 ) / b;
    return quotient;
}
```

This is how a call would have been made to this function:

```
float quotient;
quotient = divide ( 5, 3 );
```

Since the function accepts two integers, **5** and **3** are passed as arguments. The divide function receives these arguments as parameters into integer variables **a** and **b**. The function then returns the quotient which is received by the **quotient** variable.

Note: The number and type of parameters passed when making a function call should match the number and type of parameters in the function definition.

If you want to display the return value without storing it into a variable, you can call the function in conjunction with a **cout** statement as long as the returned value is displayable in nature. Here is how you display the value returned by the **divide** function directly using a **cout** statement:

```
cout << "Quotient: " << divide ( 44 , 5 );
```

Let us put *display_message*, *display_sum* and *divide* functions in a C++ code and make different calls to them in order to demonstrate the usage of functions:

```cpp
#include <iostream>

using namespace std;

//Optional function prototyping
float divide ( int , int );
void display_sum (int , int , int );
void display_message ( );

//Definition of divide function
float divide ( int a, int b )
{
    float quotient = ( a * 1.0 ) / b;
    return quotient;
}
//Definition of display_sum function
void display_sum (int x , int y , int z )
{
    cout << endl << "Sum: " << ( x + y + z ) << endl;
}
//Definition of display_message function
void display_message ( )
{
    cout << endl << "Hello! We are inside
    display_message function block! " << endl;
}
//main() function
int main ()
{
    //Declare a variable to store quotient
    float quotient;
    cout << endl << endl
        << "We are inside the main () funciton.
        Calling display_message:" << endl ;
    //Call display_message function
    display_message ();
    //Call display_sum function, pass some values
    cout << endl << endl
```

```
    << "Calling display_sum function, passing 4,
    7, 18. " << endl ;
display_sum (4, 7, 18);
//Call divide function, pass some values and
//Receive the returned value in quotient variable
cout << endl << endl
    << "Calling divide function. " << endl ;
    quotient = divide (15, 7);
//Display quotient
cout << endl << "Passed 15 and 7 to divide;
Quotient: " << quotient
<< endl ;
//Call divide directly with cout
cout << endl << "Calling divide directly with
cout: "
    << endl << "Passing 23 and 9: " << divide (
    23, 9) << endl;

    return 0;

}
```

Output:

While passing values to a function as arguments, there are three methods – pass by value, pass by reference and pass by pointer. We will look at pass by value and pass by reference in this chapter and pass by pointer will be explained in the **Pointers** chapter.

9.2.1 Pass by Value

With this method, the value of the variable is passed to the function. In the function definition, the passed values are accepted in different variables. Hence, any changes made to the received variable in the function definition do not reflect back to the calling function. The examples explained so far were using pass by value method.

Here is an example which accepts a float value, multiplies itself by 10 and returns the new value:

```
float multiply_by_10 ( float num )
{
    num = num * 10;
    return num;
}

Function call:

float number = 1.2 ;
float x = multiply_by_10 ( number );
```

In the function call, a float variable called **number** having a value of **1.2** is passed to the function **multiply_by_10**. Inside the function, there is a parameter called **num** which receives this value, in the body of the function, the value of this variable is increased by a factor of 10 and returned back to the calling function. Because pass by value method is used to call the function, the value of **number** will be unaltered in the calling function.

9.2.2 Pass by Reference

In this method, when a value is passed to a function, it is received in the function using a reference variable. A reference variable in a function definition is denoted by a prefixed **ampersand symbol (&)**. Any changes made to those variables will be reflected back in the calling function. Rest of the procedures remain the same including the function call. Let us slightly modify the **multiply_by_10** function from the previous section:

```
void multiply_by_10 ( float &num )
{
    num = num * 10;
}
```

Any changes that are made to **num** will be reflected back in the calling function, hence there is no need to return a value.

Function call:

```
float number = 1.2 ;
multiply_by_10 ( number );
```

While making the function call, the value of the variable **number** is not passed, instead a **reference to that variable** is passed. The function definition increases the value of the parameter by a factor 10. Since pass by reference method is used, the local variable **number** will now hold a value of **12**.

In order to better understand this concept, let us write a C++ program with two functions two swap two input values. One using the pass by value method and the other with pass by reference method:

```cpp
#include <iostream>

using namespace std;

//Optional function prototyping
void swap_by_value (int, int);
void swap_by_reference (int &, int &);

void swap_by_value (int x, int y)
{
    //Swap x and y
    int temp = x ;
    x = y ;
    y = temp;
    //Display x and y
    cout << endl << endl << "Inside swap_by_value
    after swapping:"
        << endl
        << "x: " << x << " y: " << y << endl;
}
void swap_by_reference (int &x, int &y)
{
    //Swap x and y
    int temp = x ;
    x = y ;
    y = temp;
    //Display x and y
    cout << endl << endl << "Inside swap_by_reference
    after swapping:"
        << endl
        << "x: " << x << " y: " << y << endl;
}

int main ()
{
    //Declare 2 integers to accept and store user
    input
    int x, y;
    //Ask the user to enter a number
```

```cpp
cout << endl << endl
   << "Enter two numbers: " ;
//Wait for user input
cin >> x >> y ;
cout << endl << endl << "Inside main ():"
   << endl << "x: " << x << " y: " << y << endl;
//Call swap_by_value
cout << "Calling swap_by_value.";
swap_by_value ( x, y );
//Display x and y, no changes to x and y done in
main
cout << endl << endl << "Inside main () after
calling swap_by_value:"
   << endl << "x: " << x << " y: " << y << endl;
//Call swap_by_value
cout << "Calling swap_by_reference.";
swap_by_reference ( x, y );
//Display x and y
cout << endl << endl << "Inside main () after
calling swap_by_reference:"
   << endl << "x: " << x << " y: " << y << endl;
return 0;
}
```

Output:

9.3 Default Arguments

You can set certain parameters of a function to have default values. While calling a function, if the parameter which has been set as default is not passed, it's default value will be used. There are a few rules to be followed while setting default arguments:

1. Only the last parameter(s) can be set as default.

2. If a parameter has been set as default, all the following parameters must be set as default.

General syntax for setting default arguments is:

```
<return type> <function name> (<parameter 1>, ...
<parameter n> = <value>)
{
    //Function Body
}
```

Example:

Let us define a function which accepts 3 parameters, returns their product. Out of the 3 parameters, the last one will be the default argument:

```
int multiply ( int a , int b , int c = 10 )
{
    return ( a * b * c );
}
```

This function can be called by passing 2 or 3 arguments. Since the third parameter *c* is set to *10*, if two arguments are passed, the third one will be considered as *10*. If 3 arguments are passed, the last argument will override *c*'s value of *10* and the newly passed value will be considered. Let us look at a few function calls and what is going to be the outcome.

```
int x ;
//Two argument call:
x = multiply ( 2, 6 );
//x will hold the value of 2 x 6 x 10 = 120
//Three argument call:
x = multiply (1, 3, 20);
//x will hold the value of 1 x 3 x 20 = 60
```

9.4 Function Overloading

Function Overloading is a concept where there can be multiple definitions of a function. Different definitions of the same function will have the same function name but different types of arguments. Function overloading can be done in two ways:

9.4.1 Different number of Arguments

Functions can be overloaded by changing the number of arguments in each definition, so that when a call is made to the function, it is appropriately resolved and the correct function is called. Let us take an example. Let us overload a function called *sum* which accepts 2, 3 and 4 arguments in different function definitions and returns the arithmetic sum of all the parameters.

```
//Two arguments
   int sum ( int a , int b )
```

```
{
    return ( a + b );
}
    //Three arguments
    int sum ( int a , int b , int c )
{
    return ( a + b + c );
}
    //Four arguments
    int sum ( int a , int b , int c , int d )
{
    return ( a + b + c + d );
}
```

As seen, there are 3 definitions having the same name – sum but different number of arguments in each definition. Let us see how each of these functions can be called:

```
//sum with 2 arguments
int x = sum ( 4, 8 );
//sum with 3 arguments
int x = sum ( 10 , 20 , 30 );
//sum with 4 arguments
int x = sum ( 150, 690, 55, 340 );
```

9.4.2 Different types of Arguments

Functions can be overloaded by changing the types of parameters each definition accepts. Logically speaking, changing the data types of function parameters may have to be followed by changing the return type of the function. Different return type is not a criterion for function overloading. For example, if there are two definitions of **sum** function, one takes **two integers** and the other takes **two floats** as input parameters. The one that takes integers will return the sum as an integer. The other one will have to return a float value else the sum will lose precision. The point is, these two functions can be overloaded because they accept different types of arguments and not because they have different return types.

Let us write a small C++ code snippet of whatever we have just discussed:

```
//Two integers
int sum ( int a , int b )
{
    return ( a + b );
}
//Two floats
    float sum ( float a , float b )
{
    return ( a + b );
}
```

Calls to each of these functions are made as follows:

```
int sum_int;
float sum_float;
//Call the function that accepts two integers
sum_int = sum ( 5, 60 );
//Call the function that accepts two floats
sum_float = sum ( 50.78, 60.1 );
```

The second function definition which accepts two float values and returns a float value could have returned an integer value and still be overloaded without problems but that would be logically incorrect as there is a very high chance of the sum of two float values being a float value.

Let us take an example of function overloading that shows the real beauty of this concept. A function called *area* will be overloaded 3 times, where each definition will compute the area of circle, rectangle and a triangle with the appropriate area formulae. We know that to compute the area of a circle, only 1 parameter is needed – radius. To calculate the areas of rectangle and triangle, two arguments are needed – length & width and base & height respectively. The area function of a circle can be uniquely identified from the other two functions based on the number of arguments. To uniquely identify area functions of rectangle and triangle, we will change the data type of the input parameters.

Here is the C++ code that accomplishes whatever we have just discussed:

```cpp
#include <iostream>

using namespace std;

//Area of a circle
float area ( int radius )
{
    //Return Pi x radius x radius
    return ( 3.14 * radius * radius );
}
//Area of a triangle
float area ( int base, float height )
{
    //Return (1/2) x base x height
    return ( (1 / 2.0) * base * height );
}
//Area of a rectangle
int area ( int length, int width )
{
    //Return (length x width)
    return ( length * width );
```

```cpp
}

int main ()
{
    //Declare variables to store user inputs
    //And to store calculated areas
    int radius, base, length, width, area_rectangle;
    float height, area_circle, area_triangle;
    //Ask the user to enter the radius of a circle
    cout << endl << endl
        << "Enter the radius of a circle: ";
    //Wait for the user to enter
    cin >> radius;
    //Call area function to calculate area of a
    circle
    area_circle = area (radius);
    cout << endl
        << "Area of the Circle with Radius: " <<
        radius
        << " is: " << area_circle;

    //Ask the user to enter the base and height of a
    triangle
    cout << endl << endl
        << "Enter the base and height of a triangle:
        ";
    //Wait for the user to enter
    cin >> base >> height ;
    //Call area function to calculate area of a
    triangle
    area_triangle = area (base, height);
    cout << endl
        << "Area of the Triangle with Base: " << base
        << " Height: " << height
        << " is: " << area_triangle;

    //Ask the user to enter the length and width of a
    rectangle
    cout << endl << endl
        << "Enter the length and width of a rectangle:
        ";
    //Wait for the user to enter
    cin >> length >> width ;
    //Call area function to calculate area of a
    rectangle
    area_rectangle = area (length, width);
    cout << endl
```

```
<< "Area of the Rectangle with Length: " <<
length
<< " Width: " << width
<< " is: " << area_rectangle << endl ;

    return 0;
}
```

Output:

```
F:\cpp>g++ functionoverloading.cpp -o functionoverloading
F:\cpp>functionoverloading.exe

Enter the radius of a circle: 5
Area of the Circle with Radius: 5 is: 78.5
Enter the base and height of a triangle: 10 20
Area of the Triangle with Base: 10 Height: 20 is: 100
Enter the length and width of a rectangle: 25 30
Area of the Rectangle with Length: 25 Width: 30 is: 750
F:\cpp>
```

Function overloading is an important concept in C++ and is extensively used in object oriented programming.

10. Arrays

An array is a collection of items of the same data type. Each item is known as an element. Each element is can be accessed using its position known as the index. Array index starts at 0 and goes up to one less than the size of the array. For example, if you had an array of 10 elements, the indices would go from 0 to 9. The first element would be present at index 0 and the last element would be present at index 9. It is possible to have arrays of any data type. The general syntax of declaring an array is:

```
<data type> <variable name> [ <size> ];
eg:
int numbers [ 10 ] ;
float marks [ 5 ] ;
```

An array can be initialized during declaration with the following syntax:

```
<data type> <variable name> [ <size> ] = { <elements
separated by comma> };
eg:
int numbers [ 10 ] = { 5, 76, 243, 7, 3 , 8, 8, 1,
98, 17 };
float marks [ 5 ] = { 45.3, 958.45, 353.09, 123.764,
111.56 };
```

During initialization, the size of the array can be optionally provided. The following statements are syntactically correct and will not return any error:

int numbers [ ] = { 5, 76, 243, 7, 3 , 8, 8, 1, 98, 17 };
float marks [ ] = { 45.3, 958.45, 353.09, 123.764, 111.56 };

To access each element of an array, the access operator (*[ ]*) is used, with the index enclosed within. Let us take an example. Consider an integer array of 5 elements having the name **num**. It would be declared as follows:

int num [5];

Since the size of the array is 5, the value of index can go from 0 to 4. Let us set values of each of the elements:

num [0] = 123 ;
num [1] = 50 ;
num [2] = 79 ;
num [3] = 6072 ;
num [4] = 446 ;

The array **num** will now look like this:

num				
123	50	79	6072	446

Index ---> 0 1 2 3 4

Instead of setting each element one by one, the above array could have been initialized as follows:

int num [5] = { 123 , 50 , 79 , 6072 , 446 } ;

Loops are particularly useful when dealing with arrays. Here is a code snippet which displays the elements of **num** array one by one using a **while** loop:

```
//Initialize a variable to 0 for iterating purpose
int i = 0 ;
```

```
while ( i < 5 )
{
    //Display num [ i ]
    cout << "num[" << i << "]: " << num [ i ] << endl
    ;
    //Increment i
    i++;
}
```

Here is another example where in a *for* loop is used to fill an array with values from 1 to 10:

```
//Declare integer array
int x [ 10 ];
//For loop to run from 0 to 9
for ( int j = 0 ; j < 10 ; j ++ )
    //Fill array x
    x [ j ] = j + 1 ;
```

Let us write a C++ program which calculates the sum and average of 5 elements of a float array. These 5 elements will be entered by the user.

```
#include <iostream>

using namespace std;

int main()
{
    float values [5], avg ;
    int i , sum = 0 ;
    cout << endl << endl
    << "Enter 5 values one by one." << endl ;
    for ( i = 0 ; i < 5 ; i ++)
    {
        //Ask the user to enter value at each index
        cout << endl << "Enter value at index " << i
        << " : " ;
        //Wait for user input
        cin >> values [i];
```

```
    }
    //Calculate sum
    for ( i = 0 ; i < 5 ; i ++)
        sum += values [i];
    //Calculate average
    avg = (sum * 1.0) / 5 ;
    //Display sum and avg
    cout << endl << endl
        << "Sum: " << sum << " Avg: " << avg << endl;
    return 0;
}
```

Output:

```
F:\cpp>g++ arraysumavg.cpp -o arraysumavg

F:\cpp>arraysumavg.exe

Enter 5 values one by one.
Enter value at index 0 : 123
Enter value at index 1 : 653
Enter value at index 2 : 175
Enter value at index 3 : 978
Enter value at index 4 : 10

Sum: 1939 Avg: 387.8
F:\cpp>
```

An important property of arrays to be noted is – elements of an array are allotted sequential memory location with each element occupying the size determined by its data type.

11. Strings

A string is a sequence of characters. Technically speaking, a string is an array of characters (***char*** data type). There is also a custom data type called ***string***, which is a part of the ***std namespace***. We have already seen the basic usage of the string class in ***Section 4*** and ***Section 6***. In this section, we will look at a more conventional approach of dealing with strings, that it – strings as arrays of characters. To declare a string, we would have to declare a character array just as we would declare any other array. For example:

```
char str [10];
```

This statement will create a string of size 10. A string can be initialized in two ways:

```
char str [ ] = { 'H' , 'e' , 'l' , 'l', 'o' };
```

In the above method, we initialize each character of the string manually which is not very convenient. The following method offers a workaround this inconvenience as a string can be set directly:

```
char str [ ] = "Hello";
```

Both these methods do the exact same thing and the character array ***str*** will look like this:

str

H	e	l	l	o

Index --->   0   1   2   3   4

You cannot assign a string value to a string using the assignment operator after declaration. The following method is incorrect:

```
char str [ 10 ];
str = "Hello" ; //Will not work!
```

If you want to assign a value to a string after declaration, you can very well set each element using the access operator (*[ ]*) as explained in **Section 10** or you can use the **strcpy** function from the **cstring** header. You will have to include the **cstring** header in your code. **strcpy** is a function used to copy a string. The syntax is:

```
strcpy     (<destination     string>     ,     <source
string/constant string>);

Refer to the following example:

#include <cstring>
...
...
char str [10];
strcpy ( str , "Hello" );
```

This code snippet declares a character array of size 10. The **strcpy** function sets the value of **str** to "*Hello*".

11.1 Reading Strings as User Input

In **Section 6** we saw how to read strings using **cin** and the problems it can lead to when there is a space in a user entered string. The examples demonstrated in that section were using the **string class** and not **character array as string** but the same problem will be encountered if we use *cin* to read strings which are *character arrays*.

The following statements are logically correct but will cause the same problems explained in *Section 6* when a string containing spaces is entered:

```
char str [10];
cin >> str ;
```

If the entered string does not contain any space, the code will work perfectly fine.

The correct way of reading strings is using the *getline* function. The *cin* object of the *iostream* class has a function called *getline* which needs to be called in the following way:

```
cin.getline (<char array variable> , <size>);
```

Example:

```
char str [10];
cin.getline ( str , 10 );
```

OR

```
cin.getline ( str , sizeof (str) );
```

Using *sizeof (str)* will automatically fetch the size of *str* which is 10 according to the declaration of *str [10]* ; *sizeof (str)* appears like a function but is a built-in operator instead.

<u>*Note:*</u> When a string is initialized or read from the user (*using cin > >* or *using cin.getline*) , if the length of the string value that is set is less than the size of the array that is declared, a

NULL character having the character value of '\0' (or an integer equivalent of 0) is appended to the set value. The remaining fields of the array if any will have any random or junk values. For example, consider the following code snippet where a string of *7* characters is declared and initialized to a value *"Hello"* having 5 characters:

```
char str [7] = "Hello";
```

Array indices from *0* to *4* will be occupied by character values *'H', 'e', 'l', 'l', 'o'* respectively. Index *5* will hold '\0' and index *6* will hold a random junk value. The *str* array will look like this:

If the size of *str* was more than 7, the remaining indices would hold junk values too.

The *NULL character* '\0' is also known as *string termination character*. This character is appended to a string so that the programmer knows where a string ends.

When a string is set using *strcpy*, the termination character could either be \0 or a *negative integer equivalent*.

Here is a C++ program which reads a string from the user using the *cin.getline* function and displays it using *cout* and also character by character using a while loop. While displaying the string character by character, the program also counts the number of characters and displays the length of the string at the end:

```cpp
#include <iostream>

using namespace std;

int main ()
{
   //Declare a char array of 50 characters
   char str [50] ;
   //Declare an integer variable
   int i = 0;
   //Ask the user to enter a string:
   cout << endl << endl
      << "Enter a string: " ;
   //Wait for the user to enter
   //Read the string using cin.getline
   cin.getline (str , sizeof (str) );
   //Display the entered string using cout
   cout << endl
      << "The entered string is: " << str << endl <<
      endl ;
   cout << "Entered string is displayed using a
loop: "
      << endl << endl ;
   /* We know that the string termination character
is \0
    * Hence we iterate a while loop until we find \0
    * \0 is an equivalent of integer value 0
    * while (str[i]) will return a true value
    * as long as str[i] does not return 0
    * and the loop will go on executing
    * until \0 if found
    */
   while (str [i])
   {
      //Display each character
      cout << str [i] ;
      //Increment i to go to the next location
      //i will also count the number of characters
      //Thereby giving the length of the string
      i ++ ;
   }
```

```
//Variable i will now hold the length of the
string

cout << endl << endl
    << "Length: " << i << endl << endl ;
  return 0;
}
```

Output:

Apart from strcpy, here are a few more useful functions provided by the **< cstring >** *header*:

```
//Returns the length of a string:
strlen ( <string> );
//Concatenates two strings
strcat ( <destination string> , <source string> );
//Compares two strings, returns 0 if equal:
strcmp ( <string 1> , <string 2> );
//Searches for a given character, returns the
location of the first occurrence:
strchr ( <string> , <char value> );
//Searches for a given character, returns the
location of the last occurrence:
strrchr ( <string> , <char value> );
```

11. Strings

12. Pointers

Pointers are special kind of variables that are used to store addresses of other variables. When a variable is declared, the system allots it some space in the memory according to its data type in order to store the contents of the variable. This memory region has an address with which it is identified and accessed. Pointers are used to store such addresses. Because it would normally be difficult to remember the address of each memory location, we have the concept of variables in the first place. Pointers is a fairly advanced subject and hence we will only cover the basics. Developers dealing with low level system applications such as memory management, kernel module development, device driver development, etc. should know pointers extremely well.

A pointer variable is declared just like any other variable with *asterisk symbol (*)* either prefixed to the variable name or suffixed to the data type . General Syntax:

```
<data type> *<variable name>;
    OR
<data type>* <variable name>;
eg:
//Integer pointers
int *p;
int* x;
//Float pointers
float *f, *g, *h;
//Character pointer
char *c;
```

A pointer will store the address of the **_same data type_**. For example, an integer pointer will store the address of an integer variable, a float pointer will store the address of a float variable and so on. A float pointer cannot store the address of an integer variable.

In order to fetch the address of a variable, *ampersand symbol (&)* is prefixed to the variable name. Consider the following code snippet:

```
int x = 500 ;
int *ptr = &x;
```

We have an integer variable *x* which is initialized to a value of *500*. An integer pointer variable called *ptr* is declared which is going to hold the address of the variable *x* and **not the value of x (500)**. In programmatic terms, it is said *ptr* is pointing to *x*.

When *x* is declared and initialized, the system will allot some memory to store its contents (which is *500* in this case). Let us assume that this memory location has an address of *12345*. The following diagram will explain what is happening with this code:

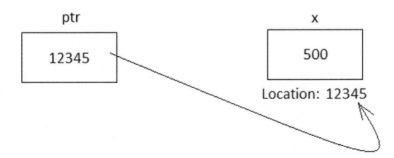

As seen, the variable *x* is holding the value of *500* and is present at memory location *12345* and pointer *ptr* is holding the address of *x* which is *12345* and not the value of *x* which is *500*. You can access the value at a memory address to which a pointer is pointing to by prefixing the **asterisk symbol (*)** to the variable name. For example: **ptr* will give you *500* and *ptr* will give you *12345*. The **asterisk symbol (*)** is used to resolve the value at a memory location. This concept is quite straight forward and confusing at the same time. This is the basic concept and if you understand it well, you can understand the whole pointers concept quite easily. Let us take a programming example wherein we shall declare a few variables and a few pointers and try to access their values:

```cpp
#include <iostream>

using namespace std;

int main ()
{
    //Declare and initialize integer vars
    int a = 10 , b = 20 ;
    //Declare and initialize float vars
    float x = 50.5 , y = 150.75 ;
    //Declare two integer pointer vars
    int *ptr1, *ptr2;
    //Declare one float pointer var
    float *fptr;
    //Assign addresses of a and b to ptr1 and ptr2
    ptr1 = &a;
    ptr2 = &b;
    //Display whatever that has been done
        cout << endl << endl
        << "a: " << a << "  --- Address of a (i.e.
        ptr1) : " << ptr1
        << endl << endl
```

```
        << "b: " << b << " --- Address of b (i.e.
    ptr2) : " << ptr2
        << endl << endl << "Value at ptr1 ( " << ptr1
        << " ) : " << *ptr1
        << endl << endl << "Value at ptr2 ( " << ptr2
        << " ) : " << *ptr2
        << endl << endl ;
//Assign address of x to fptr
fptr = &x ;
//Display whatever that has been done
    cout << endl
        << "x: " << x << " --- Address of x (i.e.
    fptr) : " << fptr
        << endl << endl << "y: " << y
        << endl << endl << "Value at fptr ( " << fptr
        << " ) : " << *fptr ;
//Assign address of y to fptr
cout << endl << endl
    << "Assigning address of y to fptr ";
fptr = &y ;
//Display fptr and y
cout << endl << endl
    << "y: " << y << " --- Address of y (i.e.
    fptr) : " << fptr
        << endl << endl << "Value at fptr ( " << fptr
        << " ) : " << *fptr ;
//Change the value of y using fptr
cout << endl << endl
    << "Changing the value of y using fptr ";
*fptr = 675.123 ;
//Display recent changes
    cout << endl << endl
        << "y: " << y << " --- Address of y (i.e.
    fptr) : " << fptr
        << endl << endl << "Value at fptr ( " << fptr
        << " ) : " << *fptr ;
cout << endl << endl ;
return 0;

}
```

Output:

```
F:\cpp>g++ pointerdemo.cpp -o pointerdemo
F:\cpp>pointerdemo.exe

a: 10 --- Address of a (i.e. ptr1) : 0x28fee0
b: 20 --- Address of b (i.e. ptr2) : 0x28fedc
Value at ptr1 ( 0x28fee0 ) : 10
Value at ptr2 ( 0x28fedc ) : 20

x: 50.5 --- Address of x (i.e. fptr) : 0x28fed8
y: 150.75
Value at fptr ( 0x28fed8 ) : 50.5
Assigning address of y to fptr
y: 150.75 --- Address of y (i.e. fptr) : 0x28fed4
Value at fptr ( 0x28fed4 ) : 150.75
Changing the value of y using fptr
y: 675.123 --- Address of y (i.e. fptr) : 0x28fed4
Value at fptr ( 0x28fed4 ) : 675.123

F:\cpp>_
```

Addresses displayed here are hexadecimal values.

Important points regarding pointers:

1. It is not possible to add, subtract, divide, multiply or perform any other arithmetic operation on two or more pointers.

2. It is possible to increment or decrement pointers but the value will be increased or decreased not by one but by the size of the given data type. For example, an integer occupies 4 bytes – incrementing or decrementing an integer pointer will have its value increased or decreased by 4. That is, the pointer will now point either to the next memory region (4 bytes forward in case of increment) or to the previous memory region (4 bytes backward in case of decrement).

3. You can also add or subtract values to/from a pointer. The pointer will now point to a new memory location specified by the number. Consider the following code snippet:

```
int a ;
int *p = &a ;
p = p + 4 ;
```

The pointer *p* will now point 4 memory regions ahead. Since an integer occupies *4 bytes*, *p + 4* will jump *16 bytes* ahead.

4. A pointer is just another variable with different features and also needs some space in the memory. The size of a pointer variable is twice the size of its data type. For example, an integer pointer will occupy 8 bytes.

12.1 Arrays and Pointers

When an array of size *n* is declared, *n* locations are reserved in the memory sequentially for *n* elements. Each element occupies the size according to the data type of the array. A float occupies *4 bytes*, a float array of *5 elements* would therefore occupy *4 x 5 = 20 bytes*. The array variable holds the address of the first location and thus acts as a pointer. Let us consider an integer array of 5 elements initialized as follows:

```
int numbers [ ] = { 10, 57, 82, 600, 425 };
```

Let us assume that the address of the first element (*numbers [0] = 10*) in the memory is **2000**. Since memory is allotted sequentially to an array and we know that an integer occupies *4 bytes* in the memory, we can derive the memory locations of all the remaining elements. Here is how the array is going to look in the memory:

numbers

Index -->	0	1	2	3	4
	10	57	82	600	425
Memory -->	2000	2004	2008	2012	2016

The array variable **numbers** will hold the address of the first element which is *2000*, *(numbers + 1)* will give the address of the second element which is *2004* and so on. We have seen many examples of how to access the elements of an array using the *access operator ([ ])*. Now, we will see how to access the elements of an array using pointers. If the array variable **numbers** is holding the address of the first element, using the value at address method, **numbers* should return the value at location *2000*, which is *10*; * (numbers + 1)* should return *57* and so on. Accessing the array elements with the statement **numbers [n]** is the same as * (numbers + n)*.

Here is a C++ program that demonstrates the method of accessing an array using pointers:

```
#include <iostream>

using namespace std;

int main ()
{
    /*char *str ;
    //str = new char ;
    strcpy (str,"Hello");
```

```
    cout << endl << endl
        << "str: " << str << endl << endl ;*/
    //Declare an integer array
    int x [ ] = {50, 40, 30, 20, 10 };
    //Declare an interating variable
    int i ;
    //Display array using access operator
    cout << endl << endl
        << "Displaying     the     array     using     access
        operator:"
        << endl << endl ;
    //Run the loop from 0 to 4
    for ( i = 0 ; i < 5 ; i ++)
        cout << endl << "x [" << i <<"] = " << x [i] ;
    cout << endl << endl
        << "Displaying the array using pointers:"
        << endl << endl ;
    for ( i = 0 ; i < 5 ; i ++)
        cout << endl << "*(x + " << i <<") = " << *(x
        + i )
        << " \tAddress (x + " << i <<") = " << (x +
        i);

    cout << endl << endl ;
    return 0 ;
}
```

Output:

115

12.2 Passing Pointer to a Function

In *Section 9*, we learned two methods to send values to a function – *pass by value* and *pass by reference*. In this section, we'll learn the third method – *pass by pointer*.

Pass by pointer method works like pass by reference method where in the changes made to the variables in the function definition will be reflected back in the calling function. The difference however is, instead of passing the reference to a variable, the actual memory address of the variable is passed. In order to pass the address of a variable, *ampersand sign (&)* will have to be prefixed to the variable name while calling the function and in the function definition, this address needs to be received in a pointer variable of the same data type. Here is a code snippet which demonstrates the pass by pointer method:

```
void swap ( int *a, int *b )
{
    int temp = *a ;
    *a = *b ;
    *b = temp ;
}
//Function call:
int x = 10 , y = 30 ;
swap ( &x , &y );
```

There is a swap function which accepts two *integer pointers* as parameters. In the function definition, the value at the addresses of these two variables are swapped using a temporary variable *temp*. While calling the function, the addresses of *x* and *y* are passed by prefixing the ampersand sign. After the swap function is called, *x* will hold *30* and *y* will hold *10*.

This method is particularly useful when passing arrays to a function. Array variable can be passed to a function as the address of the first element in the array and received by a function as a pointer. Any changes you make to the array in the function will be reflected back in the calling function.

13. Introduction to Object Oriented Programming

In *Object Oriented Programming (abbreviated as OOP)*, the emphasis is more on the data and less on the procedures. OOP revolves around the concept of *objects* which contain data and *functions* which access this data; with this objects can interact with one another. Object Oriented Programming in C++ is a vast topic and covering every concept is beyond the scope of this book. This section onward, we will learn the basics of OOP.

13.1 Classes and Objects

A *class* is a definition of a custom data type which can contain *variables* known as *data members* and *functions* known as *methods or member functions*. A class is merely a definition of the data format and may not contain data in itself. Member functions are used to access the data members of a class.

An *object* is an instance of a class which has its own set of *data members* and *member functions* as defined in the class. *Data members* are also referred to as *Attributes*.

Let us take a day-today example to understand this concept in a better way. Consider a class called Car. There are certain characteristics that come to our mind when we think of a car namely – manufacturer, model, engine displacement, fuel type, etc. Each instance of the class Car is a different car with its own set of attributes. Refer to the following diagram:

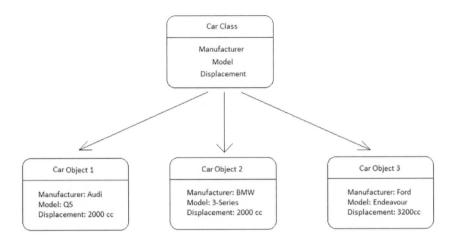

As seen from the diagram, there is a class called *Car* which has 3 data members – *Manufacturer, Model and Displacement*. Three instances (objects) of this class are created as *Car Object 1, Car Object 2 and Car Object 3*. Each object is a different car having its own values for *Manufacturer, Model and Displacement*.

If you look at this example from a programmer's point of view, the *Car Class* can have 3 data members – *Manufacturer, Model and Displacement*; to access these data members, there could be member functions, say *setData ( )* and *displayData ( )* where *setData ( )* sets each data member and *displayData ( )* displays the value of each data member.

13.1.1 Declaring Classes and Objects

A class should be declared globally so that it is accessible from any function. The syntax for declaring a class is as follows:

```
class <class name>
{
   //Data Members and Member Functions
};
eg:
class Car
{
   char Manufacturer [20], Model [20];
   int Displacement;
};
```

Class members can be declared under 3 access modifiers – *public, private and protected*. We will look at *public and private* as protected is a slightly advanced topic.

public Members:

A public member is accessible from anywhere in the program. No member functions are needed to access public members.

private Members:

Only member functions of the same class can access private members. If a member function is declared as private, only the member functions of the same class can call private member functions. This is a very important concept of data hiding in object oriented programming.

Note: Although there is no restriction of what should be public and what should be private, usually, data members are declared as private and member functions are declared as public. This is because, member functions are used to access data members of a class. If the member functions are made private, there is no way you could access them and if data members are made public, there is no need of member functions because public data members are directly accessible.

Class members declared without any access modifier are considered as private. In the above example (**Car class**), **Manufacturer, Model and Displacement** are private data members.

Let us modify the Car class to learn the syntax of declaring public and private data members:

```
class Car
{
    private:
        char Manufacturer [20], Model [20];
        int Displacement;
    public:
        void setData ( const char *, const char * ,
        int) ;
        void displayData ( ) ;
};
```

When declaring member functions, usually a function prototype is declared. You can define the function then and there within the class definition itself but it is not recommended. The preferred way of defining the declared function is outside the class. The syntax to do so is:

```
<return type> <class name> :: <function name> (
<parameters> )
{
    //Statements
```

}

Let us define the **setData and displayData** functions which sets and displays the values of ***Manufacturer, Model and Displacement*** respectively. These data members are actually ***private*** but ***displayData and setData*** functions being members of the same class can access these values and these functions being private can be accessed from anywhere:

```
//setData accepts three parameters
void Car :: setData (const char *manufacturer, const
char *model, int displacement )
{
    //Assign the value of received parameters
    //To the data members of the class
    Displacement = displacement ;
    //Using strcpy as assignment operator cannot be
    used for string assignment
    strcpy ( Manufacturer, manufacturer );
    strcpy ( Model, model );
}

    void Car :: displayData ( )
{

    cout << endl << endl
    << "Manufacturer: " << Manufacturer << endl
    << "Model: " << Model << endl
    << "Displacement: " << Displacement << endl ;
}
```

This is just a definition and no operations on the data are performed so far. We need to declare an object of the Car class which will be an instantiation of the class and that object will have its own set of data members and member functions. To declare an object, the following syntax is used:

```
<class name> <object name>;
eg:
Car c1, c2;
```

Object declaration is like declaring any other variable of a particular data type. **Car c1, c2;** statement will create two objects **c1** and **c2** of **Car** type with their own set of data members and member functions as defined in the Car class definition. To access the attributes of an object (data members/member functions), the dot (.) operator is used as follows:

```
<object name>.<data member/member function>
```

Only public members can be accessed using the dot (.) operator.

The **setData** function need to be called separately for each of the objects. As the function accepts 3 parameters, 3 arguments need to be supplied:

```
c1.setData ( "Audi", "Q5", 2000 );
c2.setData ( "BMW", "3-Series", 2000);
```

The **displayData** function can be called as follows:

c1.displayData ( );
c2.displayData ( );

It is time to combine all these concepts and put everything into a C++ program:

```
#include <iostream>
#include <cstring> //Needed for strcpy

using namespace std;

//Class definition
class Car
{
private:
    //Private data members
    char Manufacturer [20], Model [20];
    int Displacement;
    public:
    //Public member functions
    void setData ( const char *, const char * , int)
    ;
    void displayData () ;
};

//Definition of setData function as declared in Car
class
//Accepts two character pointers as strings and one
integer
void Car :: setData (const char *manufacturer, const
char *model, int displacement )
{
    //Assign the value of received parameters
    //To the data members of the class
    Displacement = displacement ;
    //Using strcpy as assignment operator cannot be
    used for string assignment
    strcpy ( Manufacturer, manufacturer );
    strcpy ( Model, model );
}
//Definition of displayData function as declared in
Car class
void Car :: displayData ( )
{
    cout << endl << endl
        << "Manufacturer: " << Manufacturer << endl
        << "Model: " << Model << endl
        << "Displacement: " << Displacement << endl ;
}

int main ()
{
    //Create 3 objects of Car class:
```

```
Car c1, c2, c3;
//Set data for each of these objects using
setData
c1.setData ("Audi", "Q5", 2000);
c2.setData ("BMW", "3-Series", 2000);
c3.setData ("Ford", "Endeavour", 3200);
//Display data of each object
c1.displayData ();
c2.displayData ();
c3.displayData ();

cout << endl << endl ;
return 0;
}
```

Output:

For you to better relate to the concepts explained so far, the data that was set for the objects is the same as shown in the Car class diagram in *Section 13.1*.

Some important points regarding Classes and Objects:

1. Data Members are usually private and Member Functions are usually public. However, there are no hard and fast rules. If a data member is made public, it could be accessed directly

using the dot operator. Eg: *<object name>.<data member>*

2. Member functions are just like any other functions, they can accept parameters, return values, etc. They can even be overloaded (*As explained in Section 9.4*) but the correct prototype for each definition should be declared in the class definition.

3. There is a special kind of member called a static member which is common for all objects. Both data members and member functions can be static but only static member functions can access static data members. To declare a static member, static keyword is prefixed before the declaration.

14. Constructors and Destructors

A constructor is a special kind of a member function which has the same name as the class. Constructors are used to initialize data members of an object. As soon as an object is created, a constructor gets invoked. Constructors can be overloaded just like functions but they cannot return any value. Recall the class Car from **Section 13.1.1**. We will modify it to add a constructor:

```
class Car
{
    private:
        char Manufacturer [20], Model [20];
        int Displacement;
    public:
        void setData ( char *, char * , int) ;
        void displayData ( ) ;
        //Constructor Declaration:
        Car ( ) ;
};
```

As seen, constructor **Car ( )** has been prototyped inside the class definition. Let us have a sample definition:

```
Car :: Car ( )
{
    //Statements
}
```

Every time an object is created, this constructor will be invoked. In the following C++ program, I have added the definition of the **Car ( )** constructor which displays **Object**

Created! on the screen every time it is invoked. In the main function, I have created 3 objects of Car class – *c1, c2, c3*.

```cpp
#include <iostream>

using namespace std;

//Class definition
class Car
{
private:
    //Private data memebers
    char Manufacturer [20], Model [20];
    int Displacement;

public:
    static int count;
    //Public member functions
    void setData ( const char *, const char * , int)
    ;
    void displayData () ;
    //Constructor Declaration
    Car ();
};
//Constructor Definition
Car :: Car ( )
{
    cout << endl << endl
        << "Object Created! "
        << endl << endl ;
}

int main ()
{
    //Create 2 objects of Car class
    Car c1, c2, c3;
    cout << endl << endl ;
    return 0;
}
```

Output:

```
F:\cpp>g++ constructor.cpp -o constructor
F:\cpp>constructor.exe

Object Created!
Object Created!
Object Created!

F:\cpp>
```

The constructor gets invoked 3 times because 3 objects are created. Declaring an object is just like declaring any other variable. You can even declare an array of objects. Let us modify the line *Car c1, c2, c3* to *Car c [10].* This should create an array of 10 Car objects and the constructor should be invoked 10 times:

```
F:\cpp>g++ constructor.cpp -o constructor
F:\cpp>constructor.exe

Object Created!
Object Created!
Object Created!
Object Created!
Object Created!
Object Created!
Object Created!
Object Created!
Object Created!
Object Created!

F:\cpp>_
```

14.1 Parameterized Constructors

A constructor is essentially a function with special properties. A constructor can also accept parameters just like any other function. General Syntax:

<class name> :: <constructor name> (<parameters separated by comma>)

{

* //Statements*

};

When creating ab object, the required parameters as defined in the constructor definition should be passed as arguments. Refer to the following syntax:

<class name> <object name> (<parameters separated by comma>);

The number and type of parameters passed as arguments during object creation should match the number and type of parameters in the constructor definition. Let us modify the *Car ( )* constructor to accept an arbitrary integer value for demonstration purpose, let this value be assigned to the *Displacement* data member of each object when created. The first thing we have to do is to change the constructor prototype to *Car (int).*

Constructor Definition:

```
Car :: Car ( int displacement )
{
    cout << endl << endl
        << "Object Created! Setting Displacement as"
        << displacement ;
    Displacement = displacement ;
    cout << endl << endl
        << "Displacement Set: " << Displacement ;
}
```

Object creation in main function:

```
Car c1 (1000), c2 (2000), c3 (3000);
```

As seen, *1000, 2000, 3000* are passed as arguments to the constructor.

Output:

A class can have multiple constructors by the virtue of constructor overloading. When an object is created, the program tries to look for the matching constructor based on the parameters. If no match is found, the compiler will return an error and the program will not compile. For example, in the above code, there is a definition for only one constructor which accepts exactly one integer parameter. During object creation, if you simply declare objects without passing any parameters like this – *Car c1, c2, c3;* the program will look for a constructor which accepts *no arguments* which is clearly not present in our code and hence the compiler will return an error. To avoid this problem, it is always better to have a constructor that accepts no arguments and/or does no operations. Such a constructor is called *default constructor* or *do-nothing constructor*.

14.2 Constructor Overloading

Constructor Overloading works just like function overloading; i.e A class can have multiple constructors with different definitions. Constructors can be overloaded on the basis of the number of parameters and the type of parameters. Function Overloading has been covered comprehensively in *Section 9.4* hence there is no need to cover Constructor Overloading separately. However, we will take a look at an example wherein we will recall the *Car class* and have 3 different constructor definitions for it. Three different definitions will be for facilitating no parameters, 1 parameter and 3 parameters. The one with no parameters is a *default constructor*, does nothing significant in this case; the one with one parameter sets only *Displacement* and the one with 3 parameters sets *Manufacturer, Model and Displacement*.

The prototypes of the constructors will be as follows:

```
Car ( ); //No parameters
Car ( int ); //1 parameter
Car ( const char * , const char * , int ) //3
parameters
```

Here is the C++ Program:

```cpp
#include <iostream>
#include <cstring> //Needed for strcpy

using namespace std;

//Class definition
class Car
{
private:
    //Private data memebers
    char Manufacturer [20], Model [20];
    int Displacement;

public:
    static int count;
    //Public member functions
    void setData ( const char *, const char * , int)
    ;
    void displayData () ;
    //Constructor Declaration
    Car ( ); //No Arguments
    Car ( int ); //1 Argument
    Car ( const char * , const char * , int ); //3
    Arguments

};

//Constructor Definition - No Parameters - Default
Car :: Car ( )
{
    cout << endl
        << "Default Constructor invoked! ";
}
//Constructor Definition - 1 Parameter
Car :: Car ( int displacement )
{
```

```
   cout << endl
      << "Constructor with 1 argument invoked! " ;
   //Set Displacement
   Displacement = displacement ;
   cout << endl
      << "Displacement Set: " << Displacement ;
      }
//Constructor Definition with 3 parameters
Car :: Car ( const char *manufacturer, const char
*model, int displacement )
{
   cout << endl << endl
      << "Constructor with 3 arguments invoked! " ;
   //Set Manufacturer, Model, Displacement
   strcpy (Manufacturer, manufacturer);
   strcpy (Model, model);
   Displacement = displacement ;
   cout << endl
      << "Manufacturer Set: " << Manufacturer <<
      endl
      << "Model Set: " << Model << endl
      << "Displacement Set: " << Displacement <<
      endl ;
}
//Definition of displayData function as declared in
Car class
void Car :: displayData ( )
{
   cout << endl << endl
      << "Manufacturer: " << Manufacturer << endl
      << "Model: " << Model << endl
      << "Displacement: " << Displacement << endl ;
}

int main ()
{
   //Create an object without passing any parameters
   //Default constructor will be invoked:
   cout << endl << endl
      << "Creating an object without passing any
      parameters:"
      << endl;
   Car c1;

   //Create an object, pass 1 integer as an argument
   //Constructor with 1 parameter will be invoked:
   cout << endl << endl
```

```
        << "Creating an object, passing 1 parameter:"
        << endl;
    Car c2 (1000);

    //Create an object, pass 3 parameters as
    arguments
    //Default constructor will be invoked:
    cout << endl << endl
        << "Creating an object, passing 3
        parameters:";
    Car c3 ("Jaguar", "XE", 1990);

    cout << endl << endl ;
    return 0;
}
```

Output:

As seen from the code and the output, 3 different objects are created with different number of arguments and the matching constructors are getting invoked appropriately.

14.3 Destructors

While a constructor gets invoked when an object is created, a destructor gets invoked when an object is deleted. Usually when a program comes to an end, all the objects that were created get destroyed automatically. If the memory was dynamically allotted to an object using pointers, a destructor would get invoked when that particular object is deleted using the ***delete*** keyword. Dynamic memory allocation is an advanced topic and hence it is not covered in this book.

A Destructor has the same name as the class but with a ***tilt sign (~)*** prefixed to it. It needs to be prototyped and defined just as a Constructor, the following syntax should be used:

```
//Destructor Prototype:
~<Class/Destructor Name> ( );
//Destructor Definition:
<Class Name> :: ~<Class Destructor Name> ( )
{
    //Statements
}
```

Let us write a C++ program to demonstrate the working of a Destructor. In the following code, a class called Test is defined which has one default constructor and one destructor:

```
#include <iostream>

using namespace std;

class Test
{
    public:
        //Constructor and Destructor Prototypes
        Test ();
        ~Test ();
};
//Construstor Definition
Test :: Test ()
{
```

```
        cout << endl << "Object Created, Constructor
    Invoked!";
}
//Destructor Definition
Test :: ~Test ()
{
        cout <<    "Object    Destroyed,    Destructor
    Invoked!"
            << endl;
}
int main ()
{
    cout << endl << "Creating 2 Objects of Test
    Class."
        << "Default Constructor should get invoked.";
    //Create 2 objects
    Test t1, t2;
    cout << endl << endl << "Program coming to an
    end."
        << endl << "This is a cout statement just
        before return 0;"
        << endl << "Objects will be destroyed and
        Destructor will be invoked."
        << endl << endl;
    return 0;
}
```

Output:

15. Inheritance

Inheritance is a concept in Object Oriented Programming which allows us to derive a new class by inheriting the properties of an existing class. Properties can include data members and also member functions. The existing class is called *base class* and the new class is called *derived class*. This process allows facilitates code reusability. Instead of writing a new class all over again, we can use the properties of an existing class and write only the additional properties that are required.

Consider a class called *Person* with public data members – *FirstName, LastName and City.* The declaration would of this class is as follows:

```
class Person
{
    public:
    char FirstName [20], LastName[20], City[20];
};
```

It would look like this:

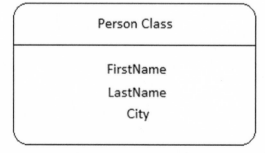

Let's say we want to declare another class called Student having the data members – *FirstName, LastName, City, School and Grade.*

The declaration would of this class is as follows:

```
class Student
{
    public:
    char  FirstName  [20],  LastName[20],  City[20],
    School[20];
    int Grade;
};
```

The Student Class would look like this:

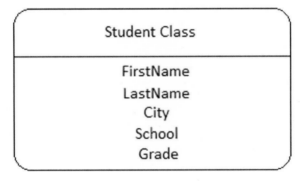

As seen from the diagrams and the code snippets, the data *members FirstName, LastName and City* are common in *Person class* as well as *Student class.* Using inheritance, we can derive the *Student class* from the *Person class* where in the *Student class* will get its own set of data members present in the *Person Class – FirstName, LastName, City* and we would have to only declare two data members inside the **Student class – School and Grade.** The general syntax for inheritance is:

```
class <Derived Class Name> : <Access Type> <Base
Class Name>
{
    //Class Definition
};
```

Only public and protected class members of a class can be inherited into another class; private class members cannot be inherited.

Access Type can be **public, private or protected.** If Access Type is:

- **public:**

    – public class members of the base class are inherited and made public in the derived class.

    – Protected class members of the base class are inherited and made protected in the derived class.

- **protected:**

    – public and protected class members of the base are inherited and made protected in the derived class.

        • **private**:

    – public and protected class members of the base class are inherited and made private in the derived class

15. Inheritance

Let use derive the Student Class from the Person Class:

```
class Student : public Person
{
    public:
    char School [20];
    int Grade;
};
```

As seen from the above code snippet, **public** inheritance is used and hence the public members of *Person class* will be inherited into the *Student class*. The Student class now has *FirstName, LastName, City, School and Grade*. This process will internally look like the one shown in the diagram below:

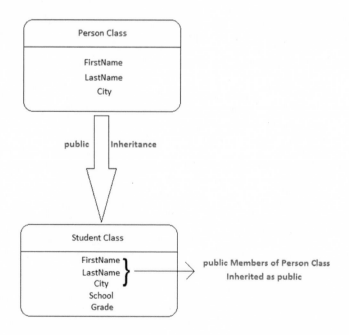

Let us write two functions *setData* and *displayData* inside the ***Student class*** and create objects of the same class inside main function to demonstrate this concept. Here is the full C++ program:

```cpp
#include <iostream>
#include <cstring>

using namespace std;

//Define base class Person
class Person
{
public:
    char FirstName [20], LastName[20], City[20];
};
//Derive Student class from Person class
class Student : public Person
{
public:
    //Additional members of Student class
    //FirstName [20], LastName[20], City[20] will be
    inherited
    char School[20];
    int Grade;
    void setData (const char *, const char *, const
    char *, const char *, int );
    void displayData ( );
};
//Function Definition of setData
void Student :: setData (const char *firstname,
const char *lastname, const char *city, const char
*school, int grade)
{
    strcpy( FirstName, firstname );
    strcpy( LastName, lastname );
    strcpy( City, city );
    strcpy( School, school );
    Grade = grade ;
}
//Function Definition for displayData
void Student :: displayData ( )
{
cout << endl << endl
```

```
            << "First Name: " << FirstName << endl
            << "Lasr Name: " << LastName << endl
            << "City: " << City << endl
            << "School: " << School << endl
            << "Grade: " << Grade << endl;
    }

    int main ()
    {
        //Create Student objects
        Student s1, s2;
        //Set data for s1 and s2
        s1.setData ("Roger", "Dimitri", "New York", "The
        Beacon School", 5);
        s2.setData ("Claire", "Smith", "Los Angeles",
        "Alverno High School", 9);
        //Display s1 and s2's data
        s1.displayData ();
        s2.displayData ();
        cout << endl << endl ;
        return 0;
    }
```

Output:

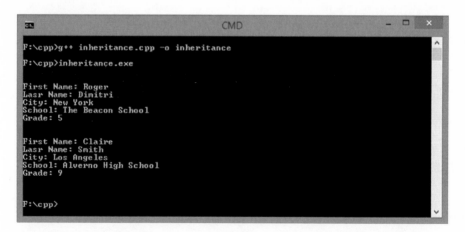

Just like public data members can be inherited, public member functions can also be inherited. Let us modify the *Person class* as follows:

```
class Person
{
   public:
   void baseClassFunction ( );
};
```

Let us define the **baseClassFunction** to display a message, nothing else:

```
void Person :: baseClassFunction ()
{
   cout << endl << endl
      << "baseClassFunction Called."
      << endl ;
}
```

Let use derive the **Student Class** from the **Person Class**:

```
class Student : public Person
{
   //Nothing here.
   //baseClassFunction will be inherited.
};
```

As seen, there is absolutely nothing inside the definition of the *Student class*. But because it is derived from the *Person class*, *baseClassFunction* will be inherited. In main function, we will declare the Student object and call the *baseClassFunction* as follows:

```
Student s ;
s.baseClassFunction ( );
```

Output:

```
F:\cpp>g++ methodinherit.cpp -o methodinherit
F:\cpp>methodinherit.exe

Calling the derived baseClassFunction using the object of the derived class.
baseClassFunction Called.

F:\cpp>
```

If there happens to be a function with the same name, same number and type of arguments in the derived class, the function from the derived class is called. This is known as *function overriding*. In this case – had there been another *baseClassFunction* in the derived class with the exact number and type of arguments, the derived class' function would have overridden the base class' function.

Constructors from the base class are also inherited by the derived class. Let us modify the Person class to include a default constructor:

```
class Person
{
    public:
    Person ( );
};
```

Let us define the base class constructor to simply display a message:

```
Person :: Person ( )
{
    cout << endl << endl
        << "Person () constructor called."
        << endl ;
```

```
}
```

Let use derive the *Student Class* from the *Person Class*:

```
class Student : public Person
{
    //Nothing here.
    //Person ( ) will be inherited.
};
```

When we declare an object of *Student class* as – *Student s*;
the *Person ()* constructor should fire up and we shall see the
following output:

In case a default constructor (or any other constructor with
the exact number and type of arguments) is present also in the
derived class, the <u>base class constructor will be called first</u> and
then the derived class constructor will be called. To demonstrate
this concept, we will modify the Student class to include its own
default constructor. Here is the full C++ code:

```
#include <iostream>

using namespace std;

//Define base class Person
class Person
{
public:
```

```
    Person ();
};
//Derive Student class from Person class
class Student : public Person
{
public:
    Student ();

};
//Define Person Class default constructor
Person :: Person ()
{
    cout << endl << endl
        << "Person () constructor called."
        << endl ;
}
//Define Student Class default constructor
Student :: Student ()
{
    cout << endl << endl
        << "Student () constructor called."
        << endl ;
}
int main ()
{
    cout << endl << endl
        << "Declaring Student class object";
    //Declare derived class object
    Student s;
    cout << endl << endl ;
    return 0;
}
```

Output:

```
F:\cpp>g++ basederivedconstr.cpp -o basederivedconstr

F:\cpp>basederivedconstr.exe

Declaring Student class object
Person () constructor called.

Student () constructor called.

F:\cpp>
```

As seen from the output, *Person ( )* constructor is called first and then the *Student ( )* constructor is called.

16. Polymorphism

Polymorphism means the ability to take multiple forms. C++ offers compile time polymorphism and run time polymorphism. Compile time polymorphism includes function overloading and operator overloading. We have covered function overloading extensively in **Section 9.4**. In this section we will learn about Operator Overloading. Run time polymorphism is an advanced topic and requires extremely well understanding of Pointers and knowledge of things like static v/s dynamic binding which is beyond the scope of this book.

16.1 Operator Overloading

In **Section 7** we have seen what kind of operators are available in C++ and how each one of them performs a specific operation. Operator overloading is concept wherein the function of an operator can be redefined to perform a different task than what the operator was originally supposed to do. For example, we know that the **addition operator (+)** performs arithmetic addition of the given numerical operands. Using operator overloading, we can redefine this operator to say add the contents of two objects.

Operator overloading is best explained with an example. Consider a class called **Test** with two private integer members **int x** and **int y**. This class has two public member functions **setData (int, int)** which sets the values of x and y and **displayData( )** which displays the values of **x** and **y**.

The class definition will look like this:

```
class Test
{
    int x, y;
    public:
    void setData (int , int);
    void displayData ();
};
```

Definitions of **setData** and **displayData** are straightforward and hence will not be covered separately.

Let us overload the **addition operator (+)** two add the contents of two Test objects. That is, if **t1** and **t2** were two objects of **Test class**, then **t1 + t2** would perform **t1.x + t2.x** and **t1.y + t2.y** and return the resulting object.

The general syntax for operator overloading is:

```
<Return      Type/Class>      operator<operator>      (
<parameters> )
    {
        //Definition
        return <Object>;
    }
```

This has to be present inside the class under public member's section.

Operator overloading boils down to defining this function. Let us see how we need to define this function for achieving our goal:

1. We know that *t1 + t2* will return another object of *Test* type hence the return type will be *Test*.

2. Left operand's (t1's) *x* and *y* will be directly accessible. Right operand will be passed as a parameter to this operator's function. Hence we will have to include a parameter of *Test* type. Let us declare that parameter as *Test Right*.

3. We will need an object of *Test* class to store the result of this addition. We will declare this object as *Test Result*.

4. Left operand's *x* needs to be added to *Right's x* and stored in *Result's y*; Left operand's *y* needs to be added to *Right's y* and stored in *Result's y*; This is done as follows:

```
Result.x = x + Right.y ;
Result.y = y + Right.y ;
```

5. Finally, the *Result* object should be returned.

Putting all these points together, we have the following operator definition:

```
Test operator+(Test Right)
{
    Test Result;
    Result.x = x + Right.x;
    Result.y = y + Right.y;
    return Result;
}
```

Here is the complete C++ program:

```
#include <iostream>
```

```
using namespace std;

class Test
{
    int x, y;
    public:
    void setData (int , int);
    void displayData ();
    //Operator + overloading as follows:
    Test operator+(Test Right)
    {
        Test Result;
        Result.x = x + Right.x;
        Result.y = y + Right.y;
        return Result;
    }

};
//setData definition
void Test :: setData (int a , int b)
{
    x = a ;
    y = b ;
}
//displayData definition
void Test :: displayData ()
{
    cout << endl << endl
        << "x: " << x << " y: " << y ;
}

int main ()
{
    //Declare two objects of Test class
    Test t1, t2;
    cout << endl << endl
        << "Setting values of t1 and t2.";
    //Set values of t1 and t2
    t1.setData (4, 5);
    t2.setData (7, 3);
    //Display values of t1 and t2
    cout << endl << endl
        << "x and y values of t1: ";
    t1.displayData ();
    cout << endl << endl
        << "x and y values of t2: ";
    t2.displayData ();
```

```
cout << endl << endl
    << "Performing t3 = t1 + t2";
//Declare new object t3 of Test class
//Perform t1 + t2
Test t3 = t1 + t2 ;
//Display values of t3
cout << endl << endl
    << "x and y values of t3: ";
t3.displayData ();
cout << endl << endl ;
return 0;
}
```

Output:

As seen from the output, x and y values of both the objects are added successfully.

Some operators can be overloaded and some cannot be overloaded.

Overload-able Operators:

+	-	*	/	%	^
&	|	!	~	=	,
<	>	<=	>=	++	--
<<	>>	==	!=	&&	||

+=	-=	/=	%=	^=	&=
|=	*=	<<=	>>=	[]	()
->	->*	new	new []	delete	delete []

Non-Overload-able Operators:

There are only a handful of operators which cannot be overloaded. They are - ., .*, ::, ?: .

Fun Fact: You may have not noticed, but we have been taking advantage of operator overloading all this while. The *left shift (< <)* and *right shift (> >)* operators are overloaded to work with ***cout*** and ***cin*** as ***insertion (< <)*** and ***extraction (> >)*** operators.

17. Programming Examples

17.1 Factorial of a number

Factorial of a number n is given by $n!$ where $n! = n \times (n - 1) \times (n - 2) \times ... \times 1$. For example, $5! = 5 \times 4 \times 3 \times 2 \times 1 = 120$. Factorial of a negative number cannot be calculated and *factorial of 0 is 1*. Mathematically, the factorial function $n!$ is also represented as $n! = n \times (n - 1)!$. Here is the complete C++ program to calculate the factorial of a number:

```cpp
#include <iostream>

using namespace std;

int main ()
{
    //Declare integers for input and for factorial
    int number , factorial = 1 ;
    //Ask the user to enter a number
    cout << endl << endl << "Enter a number: ";
    //Wait for user to enter
    cin >> number ;

    if ( number < 0 )
        cout << "Cannot compute factorial of a
        negative number! ";
    else
    {
        //Run for loop from number to 1
        for ( int i = number ; i > 0 ; i --)
            factorial = factorial * i ;
        cout << endl << endl
            << "The factorial of " << number << " is "
            << factorial;
    }

    cout << endl << endl ;
    return 0;
}
```

158

Output:

17.2 Fibonacci Series

Fibonacci series starts with the numbers *0 and 1*. The next term is obtained by adding previous two terms. The first term is 0 and the second term is 1; the third term will be 0 + 1 = 1 . Now the series will look like: 0, 1, 1. The fourth term will be 1 + 1 = 2, now the series will look like 0, 1, 1, 2. This process of deriving the Fibonacci series can go on indefinitely. Let us write a C++ program to prompt the user to enter the number of terms to be generated and then generate the Fibonacci series:

```cpp
#include <iostream>

using namespace std;

int main ()
{
    //Declare integers for input and fibo terms
    int terms , previous = 0, current = 1, next ;
    //Ask the user to enter the number of terms
```

```
cout << endl << endl << "Enter the number of
terms: ";
//Wait for user to enter
cin >> terms ;

if ( terms < 2 )
    cout << "Fibonacci series has a minimum of 2
    terms. ";
else
{
    cout << endl << endl << "Fibonacci series is
    as follows: " << endl << endl ;
    cout << previous << " " << current << " ";
    for ( int i = 0 ; i < ( terms - 2 ) ; i ++ )
    {
        //Calculate next term by adding previous 2
        terms
        next = previous + current ;
        previous = current ;
        current = next ;
        cout << current << " " ;
    }
}
cout << endl << endl ;
return 0;
}
```

Output:

```
F:\cpp\ex>g++ fibo.cpp -o fibo

F:\cpp\ex>fibo

Enter the number of terms: 10

Fibonacci series is as follows:
0 1 1 2 3 5 8 13 21 34

F:\cpp\ex>_
```

17.3 Sum of all digits of a number

Let us write a function which takes one integer variable as a parameter and returns the sum of all of its digits. To do this, the digit at one's place needs to be progressively extracted first and then discarded. This can be done by performing **number % 10** to extract the digit at one's place and then **number = number / 10** to discard the digit at one's place. Here is the full C++ program:

```cpp
#include <iostream>

using namespace std;

//Sum of digits function definition
int sum_of_digits ( int number )
{
    //Initialize sum to 0
    int sum = 0 ;
    //Loop while number is non-zero
    while ( number )
    {
        //Add one's digit to sum
        sum = sum + ( number % 10 ) ;
        //Discard one's digit
        number = number / 10 ;
    }
    //Return sum
    return sum ;
}

int main ()
{
    //Declare integer to store input
    int number ;
    //Ask the user to enter a number
    cout << endl << endl << "Enter a number: ";
    //Wait for user to enter
    cin >> number ;
    //Call sum_of_digits directly while displaying
```

```
cout << endl << endl << "Sum of all digits of "
<< number
    << " is " << sum_of_digits (number);
cout << endl << endl ;
return 0;
}
```

Output:

17.4 Reverse of a number

Let us write a function which takes one integer variable as a parameter and returns the reverse of that number; for example, if the given number is 12345, 54321 should be returned. To do this, the digit at one's place needs to be progressively extracted first and then discarded. This can be done by performing *number % 10* to extract the digit at one's place and then *number = number / 10* to discard the digit at one's place. When the digit from the one's place is extracted, *reverse = (reverse * 10) + (number % 10)* needs to be performed during each iteration. Here is the full C++ program:

```
#include <iostream>

using namespace std;

//reverse function definition
```

```cpp
int reverse ( int number )
{
    //Initialize rev to 0
    int rev = 0 ;
    //Loop while number is non-zero
    while ( number )
    {
        //Multiply 10 to rev to take it to the next
        place
        //Add one's digit to rev
        rev = (rev * 10 ) + ( number % 10 ) ;
        //Discard one's digit
        number = number / 10 ;
    }
    //Return rev
    return rev ;
}

int main ()
{
    //Declare integers for input
    int number ;
    //Ask the user to enter a number
    cout << endl << endl << "Enter a number: ";
    //Wait for user to enter
    cin >> number ;
    //Call reverse directly while displaying
    cout << endl << endl << "Reverse of " << number
        << " is " << reverse (number);
    cout << endl << endl ;
    return 0;
}
```

Output:

17.5 String Palindrome

A string is said to be a palindrome if the string and its reverse are the same. Consider a string – "madam". If you reverse the word "madam", you will still get "madam". This is a palindrome. Let us write a C++ program to take a string as an input from the user. We shall then reverse the string using a *for loop* and check if the original string and its reverse are the same using *strcmp* function (from *cstring* header). The strcmp function will return 0 if both strings are equal. Here is the C++ program:

```
#include <iostream>
#include <cstring>

using namespace std;

int main ()
{
    //Declare strings
    char str[20], reverse[20];
    //Declare integer to store the length of the
    string
    //Another integer as array index
    int length, j = 0;
    //Temporary variable for swapping purpose
    char temp;
    //Ask the user to enter a string
    cout << endl << endl << "Enter a string: ";
    //Wait for user to enter
    cin.getline (str, sizeof (str)) ;
    length = strlen (str);
    //Copy str to reverse
    strcpy (reverse , str);
    //Reverse the string, store in reverse
    for ( int i = (length - 1) ; i > ((length - 1) /
    2) ; i -- )
    {
        temp = reverse [i];
```

```
        reverse [i] = reverse [j];
        reverse [j] = temp ;
        j++;
    }
    //Display str and reverse
    cout << endl << endl
        << "Original String: " << str << endl
        << "Reverse: " << reverse << endl ;
    //Check if str and reverse are the same
    if ( strcmp ( str , reverse) == 0 )
        cout << "Palindrome: " << "YES! " ;
        else
        cout << "Palindrome: " << "NO! ";

    cout << endl << endl ;
    return 0;
}
```

Output:

18. Final Words

C++ is one of the oldest and ever evolving object oriented languages out there. Whether you are a hobbyist programmer or want to pursue a career in computer software, learning C++ will definitely give you a boost. I have covered only the basics of C++ in this book. The entire domain of C++ is vast and perhaps never ending.

If you have liked the contents of this book and have picked up the basic concepts that I have explained, I suggest you take your C++ skills to the next level by learning object oriented programming in more detail. Some of the other advanced topic you can learn are – File I/O, exception handling, dynamic memory, threading, templates/STL, etc.

Having worked with several programming languages, C++ is one of my favourites. If you obtain good command over C++, learning other object oriented programming languages such as Java, C# and Objective-C will be very easy.

Hope you have learned something of value from this book.

If you enjoyed this book as much as I've enjoyed writing it, you can subscribe* to my email list for exclusive content and sneak peaks of my future books.

Click the link below:
http://eepurl.com/du_L4n

OR
Use the QR Code:

(*Must be 13 years or older to subscribe)

Made in United States
North Haven, CT
09 September 2024

57178817R00105